Byron Nelson

The Story of Golf's Finest Gentleman and
The Greatest Winning Streak in History

BROADWAY

Co-published by:
The American Golfer, Inc.
135 East Putnam Avenue
Greenwich, Connecticut 06830
(203) 862-9720
FAX (203) 862-9724

Broadway Books
1540 Broadway
New York, New York 10036
(212) 354-6500

Design by:
ALL CAPS
599 Riverside Avenue
Westport, Connecticut 06880
(203) 221-1609

Film and separations by:
Typehouse Group
65 North Plains Industrial Road
Wallingford, Connecticut 06492
(203) 284-8737

ACKNOWLEDGMENTS

First and foremost, we would like to thank Byron and Peggy Nelson for their cooperation and
assistance in the production of this book.

We wish to express our sincerest appreciation to the contributing essayists for their fine efforts—
Ben Crenshaw, Dave Anderson, Tom Watson, Nick Seitz, Dan Jenkins and Ken Venturi; Sal Johnson for
his thorough research effort in compiling the detailed Appendix of Byron Nelson's golf achievements
and his exhaustive fact-checking in the Library of Congress and Ray Kinstler, who allowed us to
reproduce his magnificent painting of Byron that hangs in Golf House, the USGA's headquarters in
Far Hills, New Jersey.

A very special thanks as well to Desmond Tolhurst for his invaluable editing, fact-checking and general
input, and Carol Petro of ALL CAPS for her marvelous art direction. This book could not have been
published without their active assistance and cooperation.

Our appreciation also to Bill Shinker and Tracy Behar of Broadway Books and Jessica Nolfo of
The American Golfer.

Several organizations and individuals were responsible for providing many of the original photographs
accompanying these pages: specifically Andy Mutch, Nancy Stulack and Brett Avery of the United
States Golf Association, Roger Cleveland of Callaway Golf, Saundra Sheffer and Marge Dewey
of the Ralph W. Miller Library, The University of Texas at San Antonio/Institute of Texan Cultures,
The Boston Public Library, Joe Steranka of the PGA of America, John Morris of the PGA TOUR,
The Temple University Urban Archives, the Associated Press, Dan Jenkins, Matt Lawrence of Famous
Photography, The Bettmann Archive, Frank Christian Studios, Larry Hasak, the family of Tony Ravielli,
Mark Humphries, Steve Szurlej, *Golf Digest*, *Golfworld*, *The New York Times*, *The Miami Herald*, *The Seattle Daily
Times*, *The Knoxville News-Sentinel*, *Greensboro News & Record*, *The* (Montreal) *Gazette*, *The Spokesman-Review*,
Ridgewood Country Club, Muirfield Village Golf Club, Thornhill Country Club, Hope Valley Country
Club, Haas-Jordan Company, General Mills, Titleist and Foot-Joy Worldwide, ABC Sports, Ken Venturi
and, of course, Byron and Peggy Nelson.

For full-page bleed photographs, we would like to credit the following: UPI/Corbis Bettmann (pp. viii-ix);
Byron Nelson (pp. 16-17); *The New York Times* (pp. 58-59); and Mark Humphries (p. 160). We would also
like to credit *Golf Digest*, *The New York Times* and Byron Nelson for the swing photographs appearing in
the four-page double gatefold.

Thanks as well to the Sports Club at Las Colinas, the Salesmanship Club of Dallas, the GTE
Byron Nelson Classic and the members of the Preston Trail Golf Club for permitting us to photograph
Byron's memorabilia.

And last, but certainly not least, Scott Sayers and Chuck Rubin.

*"You can always argue who was the greatest player,
but Byron is the finest gentleman the game has ever known."*

— **KEN VENTURI**

Byron Nelson
Painting by Everett Raymond Kinstler
Collection USGA

For Peggy Nelson.

Byron Nelson

The Story of Golf's Finest Gentleman and
The Greatest Winning Streak in History

By Martin Davis

CLASSIC PHOTOS OF THE GREAT BYRON NELSON ■ FOREWORD BY BEN CRENSHAW ■ ESSAYS BY DAVE ANDERSON, TOM WATSON, NICK SEITZ AND DAN JENKINS ■ ANALYSIS BY KEN VENTURI

THE AMERICAN GOLFER
Greenwich

BROADWAY BOOKS
New York

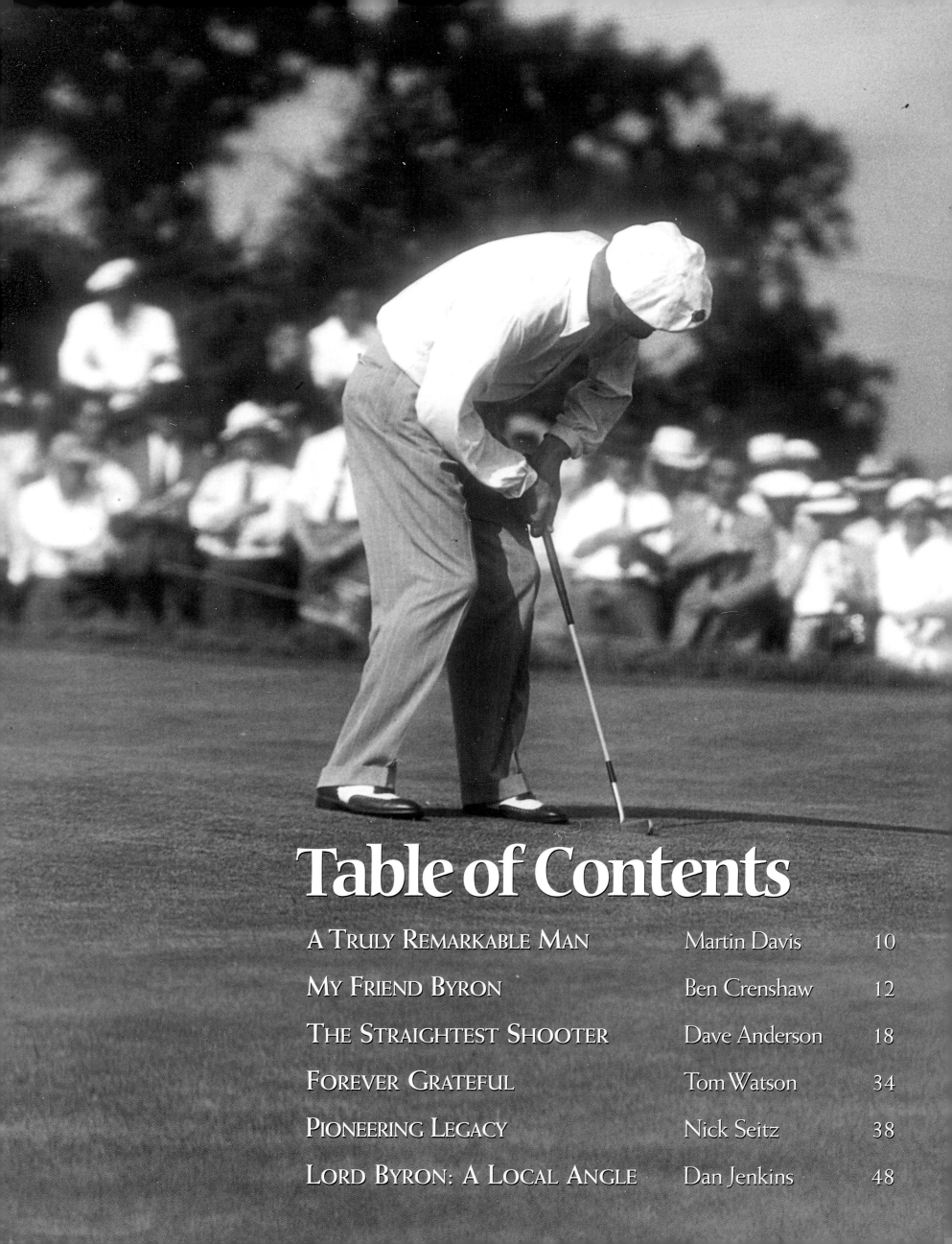

Table of Contents

Photography and Commentary

A Truly Remarkable Man

➤—•—◇—•—➤

By Martin Davis

The record amassed by Byron Nelson in his brief career before retiring at age 34 is without question the most unassailable one in all of sport.

What Byron achieved in 1945 is so incredible that it almost seems the stuff of fiction—18 tournament victories out of a total of 30 events, seven second-place finishes, 11 wins in a row, only five finishes out of either first or second (the worst a ninth place) and a 68.33-stroke average for the entire year! To place this unbelievable year in perspective, if one compares Byron's still-record stroke average with the second-place achievement of Greg Norman's 68.81 set in 1994, one realizes that Byron's record is still a full two strokes per tournament lower than Norman's—yet Byron played in twice as many events!

While preparing this book I visited with Byron during his golf tournament. As we sat in the players' dining room, all the players who entered—both great and hopeful—made it a point to pay their respects. Byron had a personal word for every single one of them. On the practice range the next day I saw Byron working with 1991 U.S. Open Champion Payne Stewart—just as Byron had with so many other wonderful players throughout the years. Interestingly, he wasn't imparting just a few random swing thoughts, but rather a thoughtful analysis of the correct swing plane.

It was clear that every player in the field respected and honored Byron greatly, and relied on the wisdom of his instruction.

In observing Byron interacting with people, it becomes obvious that it is his inner strength, his essential character if you will, that sets Byron apart—just as it was with Bob Jones. Uniquely, both set records that seem unassailable, yet it was their strength of character that set them apart.

How else can one explain the close relationship that Byron had with his pal "Jug" McSpaden—a relationship that not only survived but thrived, as McSpaden finished second to Byron eight times alone in 1945? Jug once jokingly remarked that he would have been remembered as one of golf's greats if it wasn't for Byron, yet, he named Byron as his son's godfather. This could only have come about because Byron was truly an extraordinary person and inspired a truly extraordinary friendship.

Byron clearly provides the linkage between the wooden-shafted era of Vardon, Hagen, Sarazen and Jones and the modern era of Hogan, Snead, Palmer and Nicklaus. So, it is altogether fitting that Tiger Woods won Byron's tournament this year, providing yet another link between the golf generations.

We hope you enjoy reading about this truly remarkable and wonderful man.

◀

Byron Nelson after shooting a then-course-record 66 at the 1937 Masters.

My Friend Byron

By Ben Crenshaw

ike a lot of young golfers, I grew up watching Byron Nelson doing expert commentary on ABC. However, I didn't meet him in person until 1970 when I was 18, playing as an amateur in my first U. S. Open at Hazeltine National Golf Club in Chaska, Minnesota. There I had the good fortune to make the cut, and tie for 36th place, tying another young golfer, John Mahaffey, for low amateur honors.

I remember that Byron came out to watch me for a few holes in the first couple of rounds. As always, whatever activity he was engaged in, Byron was doing his homework.

At that time, I had never seen Byron play except on TV. I had, of course seen his matches on the old *Shell's Wonderful World of Golf* shows. As you would expect, I was impressed. But, when I finally saw him hit golf shots in person, words, even my thoughts, failed me. I said to myself something like, "Oh, my goodness, look at him!" He was that good.

Even today, one must rank Byron as one of the best drivers and iron players ever to have played this game. To my way of thinking, Ben Hogan is in the same class as a ball striker, but together, Byron and Ben were simply the best ever at striking the ball. Believe me. I have seen them both.

Everyone, of course, wants to talk about Byron's streak. Many have said that doing what Byron did in 1945—winning 11 straight official tour events and a total of 18 for the year—is one of those "untouchable" records of the game. I wholeheartedly agree. That is salted away for good. It will stand forever. Jackie Burke won four in a row one time, and he told me that to do that, he literally did everything right—hit every shot, holed every putt and had every good break in the world besides. The mind boggles at 11 straight and the pitch of perfection that had to entail.

Actually, these figures, to my mind, don't tell the complete story. Two others help fill it in: His scoring average for the year—68.33—is a figure still unequalled on tour 50 years later. Even more incredible, I consider, is his finishing in the money 113 times in a row, and this at a time when tour tournaments only paid the top 20 finishers!

I'm known as a person who loves the history of the game. So, golf journalists always ask the obvious follow-up question: "Is Byron's 'year' the greatest accomplishment ever?" I have thought long and hard about that one. The answer has to be: One of the greatest? Absolutely. The greatest? I don't think you can single out just one.

While nobody will equal Byron's record, other great players have performed comparable, though different feats. In that regard, you simply can't ignore Bobby Jones' Grand Slam, Hogan's winning three legs of the modern Grand Slam in 1953 or Jack Nicklaus'

◄

A young Byron Nelson at his first Masters Tournament in 1935.

20 majors. And I could go on and on about the achievements of other great players, like Arnold Palmer and Sam Snead, to mention just two more.

In evaluating Byron's achievements, it is important to realize that he came along at a time in golf history that was one of transition in two important ways: In golf equipment, and in the role of the golf professional.

> *"I fondly remember Harvey Penick saying that Byron's divots looked like dollar bills...He had to keep the blade absolutely square for a long, long time through impact."*

Byron began playing the game with hickory shafts, but he had to adapt to the new steel shaft, which came into use early in his career. The new shafts demanded a new swing, and Byron is credited with its development, what has more lately been called the "modern swing."

If you've ever swung an old hickory-shafted club, you will have noted how the clubface opened on you going back. This opening of the clubhead came about because of the twisting or "torque" in the wooden shaft. On the downswing, you had to make an effort to roll the right hand and arm over the left to get the clubface back to square at impact. Put another way, Old Tom Morris and Young Tom Morris, Harry Vardon, Walter Hagen, Jones and other greats of the hickory shaft era didn't swing this way because they didn't know better—the shaft forced them to swing this way. And Byron had to do the same thing—he has told me that his hickory shaft swing was very loose and "handsy" in consequence.

When Byron started to play with his first steel shafts, his old swing simply didn't work any more—sheel shafts have very little torque—and gradually he put together a new swing to suit them. Now, he no longer had to manipulate the club with his hands. Instead, he kept them very quiet, allowing the body to take the club back with a rocking action of his knees. This allowed him to keep the blade square all the way back. He had a great weight shift, setting himself solidly on the right leg. Overall, he tightened up his swing, making it more of an arm swing, with the left arm being kept very straight. His top-of-swing position was now far more compact and under control. And he never overswung.

His "signature" move came in his downswing. Making far more active use of knees and feet than before, he drove his body and the club forcefully through the ball. The move was also very precise, allowing him to keep the clubface square through impact longer than anyone had done before.

I fondly remember Harvey Penick saying one time that the proof of this was that Byron's divots looked like dollar bills. Harvey further commented that, for Byron to take divots so thin, so long and so perfectly rectangular, he had to keep the blade absolutely square for a long, long time through impact.

Nobody had ever played that way before! And people said, "Golly, this guy isn't missing any shots at all!" And very often, he didn't. But, I should point out that even his misses, with that square a blade through impact, were now so much less damaging than when the blade was square for only a fraction of a second, as it had been before.

Ben Crenshaw with his friend Byron Nelson.

He had built in a margin of safety into his swing that was brand new. As an aside, I wish more young pros today would study tapes of his swing. They would learn much as well as appreciate just how good he was.

The new swing produced sensational results. A great example of this built-in accuracy was his famed 66 at his first Masters win in 1937, when he hit every par five in two, and every other green in regulation—32 shots, 34 putts—technically a perfect round. He said he didn't putt very well that day. Wow!

To think that Byron retired at 34 years old! It makes you wonder what other marvels he might have achieved if he had wanted to continue his career. But, like Bobby Jones, who also retired early, we will never know. However, it must be said that he had achieved all that he had set out to do in his career, namely win every important U.S. tournament, and he and Louise were tired of all the travelling by automobile. It was very grueling, to say the least, and one can quite understand how, after all the success he had achieved, these two simple, down-to-earth people were happy to come back home to Texas and retire to their ranch.

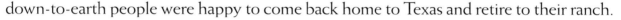

Ben Crenshaw chats with Byron and Tom Kite at Augusta in the early 1970s.

Byron was also a key figure in the development of the touring professional as we know of him today. When Byron started his career, he, like every other tournament professional of the day, considered that a good playing record was simply a way of getting a position as head professional at a fine club. As Jackie Burke told me, "The way it was back then, you played the tournament circuit just to get a job at one of those clubs."

As you will learn in later essays in this book, Byron and his good friend and "Gold Dust" twin Harold "Jug" McSpaden were among the first professionals to be able to quit their club jobs because of their contracts with golf manufacturers.

But, Byron's contributions to golf—and to life—extended far beyond mere playing ability. He has dedicated himself to service in golf and has touched every department of the game—manufacturers, club members, caddies, administrators, the people involved with his own Byron Nelson Golf Classic, they all know, they all have found that he's someone that you can count on for solid advice. And he also was very much involved in the development of two things that every golfer needs—a good solid pair of shoes and a storm-resistant umbrella!

Most important of all, Byron is a very open, very giving person. Most golfers know that he coached Ken Venturi and Tom Watson. But, he has been teacher and mentor not only to them but to countless other young players who have not achieved the fame of that pair. His is a fatherly image that has meant so much to so many. He has always found time for the young people coming along in the game. In fact, he has found time for everybody. I know that he has always given me very sound advice.

Summing up, it is Byron's personal qualities that are most important. His golf is quite overshadowed by his humanity. It is obvious that, a long time ago, he decided to do whatever was in his power to make the game better and he's done a great job doing just that. Put another way, he is probably one of the kindest men who has ever walked this planet. I am proud to call him my friend.

The Straightest Shooter

>———I———◇———I———<

By Dave Anderson

Or most golfers, shooting in the 60s is an ambition seldom, if ever, realized. But for Byron Nelson in 1945, breaking 70 was almost as easy as breaking a sweat. By late July he had won nine straight tournaments on the PGA Tour over more than four months. Two weeks earlier he had won the PGA Championship, golf's only major during that summer when World War II ended. The streak would identify him, but at the time it burdened him.

"The next week at the next tournament," he would say, "the headline was the same— 'Can Nelson Win Again?'"

In any sport, winning is always more difficult when you or your team is expected to win. Understandably, he was weary from the expectations that surrounded his every swing, his every putt. Now, on the morning of July 26 when the Tam O'Shanter tournament would start in suburban Chicago, he kissed his wife Louise as he left their hotel room.

"I hope I blow up," he told her.

When he returned several hours later, Louise asked, "Well, did you blow up?"

"Yes," he said. "I shot 66."

The next day Byron Nelson shot 68, followed by another 68 and 67 for 269, a total of 19 under par, for his 10th consecutive victory. The next weekend he would win the Canadian Open at the Thornhill Country Club in Toronto, his record 11th straight. Two weeks later the streak stopped. He tied for fourth at the Memphis (Tenn.) Invitational won by an amateur, Fred Haas, Jr.

But the streak was only the best part of Nelson's best year.

With three victories at Phoenix, Corpus Christi and New Orleans before the streak and four after it at Knoxville, Esmeralda, Seattle and Fort Worth, he won a record 18 of his 30 official PGA Tour events. He also had seven seconds, one third, two fourths, one sixth and one ninth (his lowest finish). Of those 30 tournaments, he finished over par in only two. His stroke average was 68.33, including 19 consecutive rounds in the 60s. His final-round average score was even better, 67.45. But in that era before television and before sports marketing, his only commercial reward was $200 and a case of Wheaties every month for a year.

"I like Wheaties," he said, "but I couldn't eat a case a month. I gave a lot away."'

◄

**Lawson Little and
Byron Nelson.**

His official prize money that year, in cash and in War Bonds if held to maturity, was $60,337.32.

Based on 1997 prize money, his 1945 earnings would have been worth almost $6 million.

Never before or since has a golfer been so dominant in a calendar year. Not Bobby Jones, not Walter Hagen, not Gene Sarazen, not Ben Hogan, not Sam Snead, not Arnold Palmer, not Jack Nicklaus, not Gary Player, not Lee Trevino, not Tom Watson, not Seve Ballesteros, not Nick Faldo, not Greg Norman.

"Nelson plays golf shots like a virtuoso," Tommy Armour, the golf guru of that era, once said. *"There is no type of problem he can't handle. He is the finest golfer I have ever seen."*

Not nobody.

That's how good a golfer this tall Texan with the huge hands was in the year of his streak—a year that almost any other golfer would be happy to consider a career, a year with a streak of outplaying each tournament's entire field that no other athlete has ever approached.

Joe DiMaggio hit safely in 56 consecutive games for the New York Yankees in 1941, but his .357 batting average that season was third in the American League.

Johnny Unitas threw a touchdown pass in 47 consecutive games for the Baltimore Colts, but he needed five seasons to do it (1956-1960). He also needed teammates.

Martina Navratilova won 74 consecutive tennis matches while winning 13 tournaments in 1984, but she had to conquer only seven opponents in major tournaments, only six or five in the others.

Wilt Chamberlain averaged 50.4 points a game for the 1961-62 Philadelphia Warriors, but the Boston Celtics won the National Basketball Association championship.

Rocky Marciano retired undefeated in 1956 as the world heavyweight champion with 49 victories, including 43 knockouts, but he boxed as a professional for nine years.

Byron Nelson did it all in one year and all by himself in a game without any defense. If somebody else was hot, he had to be hotter. But 1945 was merely the best of his many big years. His career total of 52 official PGA Tour victories ranks fifth, behind Snead's 81, Nicklaus' 70, Hogan's 63 and Palmer's 60. Those four were out there for anywhere from 20 to 30 years. He was out there for only a dozen years.

"Nelson plays golf shots like a virtuoso," Tommy Armour, the golf guru of that era, once said. "There is no type of problem he can't handle. High shots, low shots, with the wind and across it, hooks or fades—he has absolute control

Tommy Armour with the British Open trophy.

of all of them. He is the finest golfer I have ever seen."

Armour, the silver-haired Scot who won the 1927 U.S. Open at Oakmont and the 1931 British Open at Carnoustie, saw Bobby Jones at his best and, in their informal matches, accepted a stroke a side from Jones because "that's how goddam good he was." But when Nelson was at his best, Armour thought he was better than Jones or anybody else. Armour never saw much of Nicklaus but in 1952, several years after Nelson was at his best, the golfer known as Lord Byron gave a clinic that Nicklaus attended.

"I never saw Byron play except for that clinic," the Golden Bear would say later, "but that was the straightest hitting of a golf ball I've ever seen."

In life, Byron Nelson has been even straighter. The son of a Bible-scholar mother, he's a model for the Church of Christ teachings. He's never been heard to use bad language. He's had maybe a dozen drinks. He's never smoked. When he signed a six-month $500 contract in 1936 to appear in advertisements for 20 Grand cigarettes, he didn't realize it would produce a rash of letters from Sunday-school teachers, among others, chastising him for not being a good role model.

Byron, age five, with his mother at his Grandmother Allen's home in Waxahachie, Texas.

"I talked to the 20 Grand people and told them I'd give the money back if they'd stop the ad, but they couldn't or wouldn't," he later acknowledged. "I promised the good Lord if He'd forgive me I'd never let anyone else down and try to be a good example, and I've worked very hard at doing that."

He succeeded. One of his golf pupils, Ken Venturi, the longtime CBS television analyst who won the 1964 United States Open before a hand injury shortened his career, remembered when they were together on a West Coast tour of exhibition matches. At every stop, Nelson always had two questions.

"What's the course record?" he would ask. "And who owns it?"

One day Venturi asked Nelson why he asked those two questions.

"If the home pro owns the course record, you don't break it," he explained. "The home pro lives there. We're just visitors."

That tells you all you need to know about why Byron Nelson has a reputation others envy.

Even though Byron was one of the straightest drivers in golf history, he occasionally ended up in the rough.

"If whenever people mention great players, they think of Nelson too, that would be nice," he once said, "but I prefer being remembered as a nice man with a lot of integrity, as somebody people could love and trust, as being friendly and a good Christian man. I don't think I know anybody who has as many friends as I do. It's very gratifying. If I had made $20 million when I played golf, I probably wouldn't be as good of a man as I am now. If I made all the money in the world, my life wouldn't have been improved on."

And as a golfer, what he did in 1945 is not likely to be improved on, or even approached.

"I never dreamed of anything like that," he has said of that year. "The mechanics of my swing were such that no thought was required. It's like eating. You don't think to feed yourself. All my concentration was on the scoring, not the swing, so I'll never know what caused it. The main thing I worried about was my tempo. When galleries start running down the fairway, rushing and shoving, you unconsciously quicken your stride. Some call it timing. I call it tempo and it's everything. I was afraid of losing it, but I couldn't lose it."

What he did lose, partly because of the burden of his 1945 dominance, was his desire to keep playing tournament golf.

By the end of the 1946 season he had saved enough money to buy what he would name Fairway Ranch in Roanoke, Texas, just up state highway 114 from what is now the Dallas-Fort Worth airport. He was not yet 35, an age when Ben Hogan, his one caddie rival at the Glen Garden Country Club in Fort Worth, had won only one major (the 1946 PGA Championship) but he had already won five—the Masters in 1937 and 1942 (in a playoff with Hogan), the 1939 United States Open and the 1940 and 1945 PGA Championships. He had won prize money in 113 consecutive events, sometimes when sponsors only paid the leading 12 or 20 golfers.

"That shows I had a very repetitive golf swing," he said proudly, "and that I never got disgusted and quit trying."

His swing was so repetitive, even his divots were repetitive. The late Harvey Penick, the legendary teaching pro at the Austin (Texas) Country Club, watched him develop from a promising amateur into a prosperous pro.

"Byron had a lateral shift," Penick wrote in his *Little Red Book*, "which I believe helped him in getting a thin divot that looked like a dollar bill— one of the few I ever saw in that precise shape."

His swing was so smooth that even on his occasional returns to competition just for the fun of it, he won twice—the 1951 Bing Crosby National Pro-Am and the 1955 French Open. When the United States Golf Association later created a mechanical golfer to test equipment at its Far Hills, N.J., headquarters, it was named "Iron Byron."

Had he continued to compete, or had the U.S. Open and the Masters been held during World War II, how many more majors would he have won? How many more PGA Tour events?

"I've never looked back," he often said. "Nobody understands it, but I never did feel I quit too soon. I accomplished everything I set out to do. People say it's too bad that I won all those tournaments and the prize money was so small. I'm not

The first trophy Byron ever won was at Katy Lake in 1928.

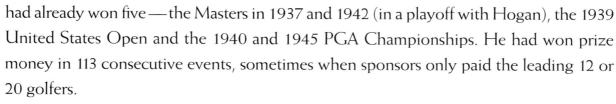

Byron at work at his ranch.

Bing Crosby congratulates the "retired" Byron Nelson on winning the 1951 Crosby Pro-Am at Pebble Beach.

envious. It was fun playing when I played, and I don't think it's so much fun now. I had been under a lot of pressure and I knew I was going to be a rancher."

Even with all the money he earned in 1945 his wife Louise delayed the purchase of the ranch.

"I didn't want him to have a ranch," she said several years before her death in 1985, four months after their 50th wedding anniversary. "He didn't know anything about ranching and I was afraid he would lose everything he had worked so hard for. Finally I said, 'All right, but you can't touch any of our investments. You have to earn every bit of it.' I said, 'I've got both feet in concrete and I'm not changing. We've worked hard and I'm afraid you'll lose it ranching.' Looking back on it, I realize I was being selfish, but anyway he got himself busy and won a lot of money. That was

Above and left: Iron Byron, the USGA's testing machine, is patterned after Byron's swing.

1945. When he had saved up over $50,000 in cash, he thought he could start looking. But it wasn't enough money and I said, 'Well, you're just going to have to work another year. You'll have to work through the National Open.' We made a pact we wouldn't tell anyone and we didn't. He almost won that Open."

After 36 holes of that Open at the Canterbury Country Club outside Cleveland, Nelson was only two strokes behind Hogan and Vic Ghezzi. In those years before roped-off fairways the Open's final 36 holes were played on Saturday in morning and afternoon rounds.

That morning most of the 12,000 spectators were in Nelson's gallery, restrained only by ropes held by the marshals. On the 13th hole, a par five, Nelson's second shot stopped near the green as his gallery surged up the fairway close to the ball. So close that when Nelson's caddie, Eddie Martin, who was on an Army furlough, ducked under the marshal's rope, he lost his balance, stumbled and accidentally kicked Nelson's ball about a foot. Penalty stroke.

Even so, his 69 lifted him into the 54-hole lead at 211 going into the final round in the afternoon, a stroke ahead of Lloyd Mangrum and Ghezzi, two ahead of Hogan. In the afternoon, Ghezzi was already in the clubhouse with 284 when Nelson arrived at the 16th tee needing three pars for 282.

Lloyd Mangrum with Byron and Vic Ghezzi before the playoff for the 1946 U.S. Open.

After a par at the 16th, Nelson bogeyed the 17th when he missed a three-footer. On the 18th, he hooked his drive, left his second shot short of the green and took another bogey for 284, tying Ghezzi. Mangrum also finished at 284, forcing a three-man playoff the next day. When each shot 72, another 18-hole playoff was required. Mangrum won with a 72, a stroke ahead of both Nelson and Ghezzi.

Another golfer might have blamed his caddie, the gallery or the marshals for the penalty stroke that theoretically created the playoff, but Nelson never did.

COMPLIMENTS OF BYRON NELSON

Byron sank this putt on the 18th green at the 1946 San Francisco Open at Olympic to win by nine shots.

Typically, he blamed himself for waiting for a ruling when he finished that morning round instead of accepting the penalty stroke immediately.

"Ike Grainger," he wrote in his autobiography, *How I Played the Game*, referring to a USGA official, "preferred to talk to the committee before he made a ruling, though he said I had the right to have a decision right then. I said it was O.K. to wait, which was my mistake. And in my mind, that's what cost me the tournament. Not the delay itself. I was trying to play with all that on my mind. I was pretty sure I would receive a penalty stroke, but not having it settled right there, I played two over par from there in and then had the penalty stroke added on."

In retrospect, maybe the penalty stroke wasn't as decisive as his lack of concentration after having opened 1946 with successive victories in the Los Angeles Open and the San Francisco Open.

"The focus of needing more money for the ranch lasted until that San Francisco Open," he later said of a tournament he won by nine strokes. "But the day after that tournament, it was gone."

Suddenly Byron Nelson was gone too. Gone to Roanoke, Texas, to pay $82 an acre for the 750-acre cattle ranch he always wanted: the long asphalt driveway to dozens of huge live oaks and a huge hackberry surrounding a two-story white-trimmed brown-shingled brick ranch house embraced by flowers. Gone to what wasn't that much different from his roots, a 160-acre cotton farm in Long Branch, Texas, just outside Waxahachie, where he was born on February 4, 1912. At first, the doctor thought 12-pound 8-ounce John Byron Nelson, Jr. was dead as he struggled to save Madge Allen Nelson's life. In a difficult delivery, the doctor's forceps had broken the baby's nose and dented his forehead. But his maternal grandmother noticed movement.

When Byron retired in the fall of 1946, the mayor of Denton, Texas, presented Byron and Louise with two half-Tennessee Walkers.

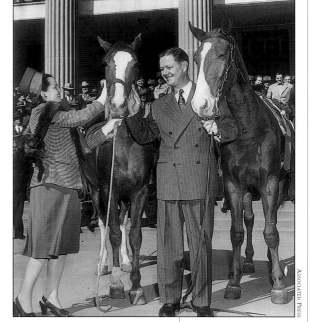

ASSOCIATED PRESS

COMPLIMENTS OF BYRON NELSON

Byron at six months of age in 1912.

"Doctor," she yelled, "this child is alive and active."

Alive and active. As a little boy, he was feeding one of his father's horses an ear of corn when the horse bit off the tip of his left forefinger. At six, his family moved to a 240-acre cotton farm on the San Saba River in southwest Texas, where he rode a horse bareback three miles to and from school. When he was seven, his sister Ellen was born. Seven years later, their brother Charles arrived. By then he had survived another death scare, typhoid fever, and the family was living in Fort Worth, about a mile from the Glen Garden Country Club where some of his friends caddied.

"They had money in their pocket, not much money, but something," he recalled. "I wanted something in my pocket too."

At the annual caddie Christmas tournament a few weeks later, he borrowed a set of clubs and shot 118. Soon he bought an old hickory-shafted mashie, what is now a 5-iron. He learned to hit old balls with it when he wasn't watching how the better golfers swung. In the 1927 nine-hole caddie championship he sank a long putt on the last green to tie another Glen Garden caddie, little Ben Hogan. Each had shot 40, three over par, in the prelude of four other duels as pros. In their Glen Garden play-

off, Nelson won by a shot. His prize was a 5-iron, Hogan's a 2-iron.

Byron, age 10 (fifth row, third from right), in "Miss Bonnie's" fifth-grade class.

"I already had a 5, and Ben already had a 2," he recalled, "so we traded clubs."

Earlier in 1927 he went to his first big golf tournament, accompanying the Glen Garden pro, Ted Longworth, to the PGA Championship over in Dallas at the Cedar Crest Country Club where Walter Hagen was in a 36-hole semifinal match against Al Espinosa. With no gallery ropes, he was able to stay with Hagen almost step-for-step. On the final nine, Hagen, who was about to address an approach shot, kept squinting into the slanting sun.

In the 1927 PGA Championship, Byron, as a child, had loaned Walter Hagen his cap to shield his eyes from the sun; Hagen went on to win his record fifth PGA. In an interesting quirk of fate, Byron was named to the 1941 Ryder Cup Team captained by Hagen. Alas, the 1941 Matches were not played because of the continuation of World War II.

"Would you like to borrow my cap?" Byron asked.

Hagen glanced at him, smiled and said, "Yes."

With the peak of Nelson's cap shading his eyes, Hagen hit his approach about eight feet from the cup, then handed the cap back to the skinny kid in his gallery. Hagen sank that birdie putt and eliminated Espinosa on the 37th hole. The next day Hagen won his fifth PGA title, 1 up, over Joe Turnesa.

"You'd think I would've kept that cap all this time, but I haven't," Nelson has said. "I've never kept clubs or balls I won tournaments with or anything like that. Just not sentimental that way, I guess."

Beginning in 1935, however, he had kept a record of his tournament scores, finishes and earnings, what would be published in 1995 as his *"Little Black Book."* But in his Fairway Ranch home, there are no clubs or balls. Only a trophy or two and a few golf photos are on display, no-tably a framed photo of a lean young pro in a tie and shirt swinging a golf club, his arms extended, his head behind the ball, his body beautifully balanced.

Byron's original *Little Black Book.*

"I don't know about you," he once told Larry Dorman of *The New York Times* while staring at that photo, "but I don't see anything at all wrong with that swing."

Even so, that swing needed time. As a teenager he was working in the Glen Garden pro shop, mowing the greens, and selling the eggs from the chickens on his family's farm while reading Harry Vardon's instructional book and playing as much golf as he could. When he dropped out of school in the 10th grade, he worked for the Fort Worth and he has called his "only regret" in life.

"I didn't allow her," he said years later, "to adopt a couple of children when she wanted to."

They had hoped for natural children, but when Louise couldn't get pregnant, medical tests showed that his childhood siege with typhoid fever had left him sterile. He didn't want to risk the problems he had seen develop in other families with adopted children, especially with all the traveling he had to do.

The flagpole Byron hit at the Ridgewood Country Club.

On his return to Ridgewood with his reshaped driver, Nelson adjusted his swing to what was then a high-tech innovation: steel shafts.

"You had to be more upright," he said. "You had to use your feet and legs more. You had to take the club straight back and inside."

He began hitting the ball so straight that one day he accepted a challenge from the Ridgewood caddies. They bet he couldn't hit the flagpole across the putting green with a 3-iron off the slate patio in front of the pro shop, a distance of nearly 100 yards. The caddies put up nickels and dimes, about 55 cents in all.

"My first shot faded a little, it missed by six inches," he recalled with a smile. "I drew the second shot. Bang."

He soon won the New Jersey Open and the next year, at Quaker Ridge, he won the Met Open, then considered a major with a prestigious national field (Horton Smith, Paul Runyan, Denny Shute, Craig Wood). That fall he finished third in the Western Open, also considered a major then, and went on to play in St. Paul, Vancouver, Victoria, Seattle and Portland, earning nearly $2,600.

Byron won the Western Open at Medinah in 1939.

"From then on," he has said, "I never looked back and never tried to change anything in my swing. I don't mean to boast. I mean, I was in contention from then on."

In the 1937 Masters, he leaped from contention to champion. In the final round, he trailed Ralph Guldahl, who would win the U.S. Open that year and the next year, by three shots going to the back nine. When Guldahl birdied the 10th, Nelson knew he needed a 12-foot putt in order not to drop four behind. He made it. At the short 12th, Guldahl took a double-bogey 5, then had a bogey 6 on the dogleg 13th. Minutes later on those same holes Nelson had a birdie 2 and an eagle 3, a swing of six strokes and a two-shot lead for his first major.

"But the birdie at 12 and the eagle at 13 were set up by the birdie on 10," he has said. "When I made that putt, Wiffy Cox told me, 'Kid, I think that's the one we needed.' And it was. That was the biggest putt I ever made. That victory means the most."

That victory at the Masters also prompted his "Lord Byron" nickname. O.B. Keeler, *The Atlanta Journal* golf writer and confidante of Bobby Jones, dubbed him that because the way he played the back nine had reminded

"Two things were repeated too often—poor chipping and careless shots...So I made up my mind... for all of 1945 I would try very hard to avoid a careless shot...I wanted to establish some records that would stand for a long time."

Keeler of a poem written by Byron when Napoleon was defeated at Waterloo. The connection was more than Keeler realized.

"My father," Nelson has said, "was named Byron because his mother loved the poetry of Lord Byron. Although my father didn't use that name, I was named after him, and I love the name."

While head professional at Inverness, Byron played an exhibition game for the Toledo Mudhens against the St. Louis Browns. He is shown here with Mudhens' manager Fred Haney.

In the 1939 U.S. Open at the Philadelphia Country Club's Spring Mill course, Nelson came from behind again. After the Saturday morning round, he was at 216, five shots behind Johnny Bulla, four behind Sam Snead, Denny Shute and Craig Wood, and two behind Olin Dutra, with whom he was paired. At lunch in the clubhouse before the afternoon finale, Dutra, the 1934 U.S. Open champion, ordered roast beef with gravy.

"I'll have that too," Nelson said.

Sitting with them, his Texarkana friend, J.K. Wadley, barked, "No, you don't. You eat a chicken sandwich with a touch of mayonnaise on it and a vegetable on the side. You don't need to go out there all logged down and half asleep because you ate too much." Nelson changed his order.

Logged down or not, Dutra shot 78. Nelson shot 68 for 284, the leader in the clubhouse after a birdie on the 17th.

Out on the course, Snead needed only to par the last two holes for a 70 and 282. But he bogeyed the 17th, then took a triple-bogey 8 on the final hole for 286.

Shute now needed only two pars for 283, but he bogeyed the 17th and finished at 284. So did Wood, with a birdie on the 18th, forcing a three-way playoff. The next day Nelson and Wood each shot 68 as Shute skied to a 76. Needing an eight-foot putt on the 18th hole for a birdie and a second 18-hole playoff, Byron later said "I thought back to Glen Garden when we would talk about having this putt or that putt for the National Open, so that thought popped into my mind as I was standing over that putt. I hit it and knocked it in."

Nelson was the pro at Inverness in 1940. On the floor to his right is the Vardon Trophy which he won in 1939.

> "*Of his first nine tournaments in 1945, he won three and finished second in five. And then the streak began, the streak remarkable not only for his winning but for his winning margin.*"

In the second 18-hole play-off the following day Nelson jumped into a one-stroke lead on the third hole. At the dog-leg-right 453-yard fourth, he hit a perfect drive, then smoked a 1-iron that landed in front of the green and rolled into the cup. Eagle 2.

"It startled me in a way," he said later. "I made a bogey on the next hole, so I said to myself, 'Don't let it bother you that you made an unusual shot. Just forget about what happened.' I steadied down and played steady for the rest of the day."

He won with a 70 to Wood's 73, but he would often be asked if he resented people remembering that 1939 Open for Sam Snead losing it with that 8 (hooked tee shot into the rough, topped 2-wood into a fairway bunker, 8-iron into seams of sod, a blast into another bunker short of green, pitched onto green, three putts) rather than for his winning it.

"No, and I'll tell you why," Nelson has always said. "I think the record would prove that most Opens are lost rather than won. And it's just that Sam never won the Open and that's why they remember him losing the Open that I won."

In their 36-hole final for the 1940 PGA Championship, Snead didn't lose it. Nelson won it. One down after 33 holes, he holed a six-footer for birdie to square the match, sank a three-footer for another birdie to go 1 up, then rifled a 3-iron to 10 feet behind the flagstick. When Snead missed his 25-foot birdie chance, Nelson eased his down-hill putt near the cup, then tapped in to win.

And at the 1942 Masters, Hogan didn't lose it. Nelson won it despite having thrown up during the night in his hotel room.

Hogan suggested the 18-hole playoff be postponed until later in the day, but Nelson insisted they tee off on time. "That wasn't as noble of me as you might think," he has said.

"The upset-stomach business had happened to me before and every time I had been in a keyed-up, nervous condition, I had played rather well." But with a double-bogey at the first hole after pushing his drive into the pine trees and a bogey at the fourth, he dropped three strokes behind.

"Somewhere around the fifth, my adrenaline glands started to going and pretty soon I felt just as strong as I could be," he re-

To aid in the War effort, Byron toured with the Red Cross and USO tours in 1942-43. Pictured here are Bob Hope, Bing Crosby, Byron, Johnny Weissmuller and Jimmy Demaret.

WARNER BROS.

Byron posed for a publicity shot with some starlets at the Hillcrest Country Club in Los Angeles. The woman on Byron's left is Georgia Carroll, a very popular fashion model of the day.

MERCHANTS PHOTO SERVICE

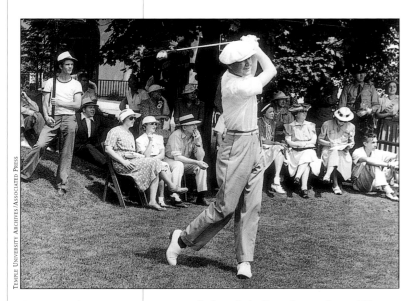

Byron at the 1939 PGA Championship at Pomonok.

called. "I had that old spring in my arms and legs."

Nelson birdied the short sixth (as Hogan bogeyed), eagled the eighth (as Hogan birdied) to draw even. On the back nine he birdied Amen Corner (the 11th, 12th and 13th). He had 69, Hogan 70.

By then, four months after Pearl Harbor, some touring pros were on their way into military service. Nelson was classified 4F; his blood didn't coagulate normally. To do his part in the war effort, he toured military bases with Bob Hope, Bing Crosby and Johnny Weissmuller, and also played War Bond exhibitions with Jug McSpaden, also 4F because of severe allergies and sinusitis, in addition to his tour events. Of the 23 official PGA Tour events in 1944 he won eight (plus three unofficial events), but he was haunted by 10 second-place or third-place finishes, especially his 1-up loss to Bob Hamilton in the PGA final.

"In looking over the book I kept that year, I found two things that were repeated too often—poor chipping and careless shot," he wrote in his autobiography. "So I made up my mind, like a New Year's resolution, that for all of 1945 I would try very hard to avoid a careless shot. Having the extra incentive of buying a ranch made things a lot more interesting and I wanted to establish some records that would stand for a long time."

Of his first nine tournaments in 1945, he won three and finished second in five. And then the streak began, the streak remarkable not only for his winning but for his winning margin.

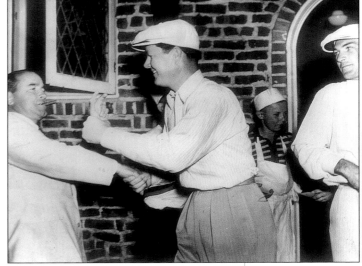

Byron playfully cuffs Gene Sarazen at Cherry Hills after defeating Ben Hogan (right) 2 and 1 in the quarterfinals of the 1941 PGA Championship.

Byron plays an iron down the seventh fairway in the qualifying round of the 1944 PGA Championship at Spokane, Washington. He was runner-up of the day with a round of 70.

In the Miami Four-Ball, he and McSpaden defeated Willie Klein and Otey Crisman, 6 and 5, in the opening round, Ben Hogan and Ed Dudley, 4 and 3, in the second round, then eliminated Henry Picard and Johnny Revolta, 3 and 2, in the semifinals before routing Denny Shute and Sam Byrd, 8 and 6, in the final. On to Charlotte where he edged Snead by four shots in a 36-hole playoff, to Greensboro where he won by eight, to Durham where he won by five, to Atlanta where he won by nine, to Montreal where he won by ten, to Philadelphia where he won by two, to the Victory Open (an unofficial wartime substitute for the U.S. Open) at the Calumet Country Club outside Chicago where he won by 10, to the PGA Championship at the Moraine Country Club in Dayton, Ohio where, oops, he suddenly found himself two down with four holes to go against Mike Turnesa in their 36-hole second-round match.

But he birdied the 33rd hole, birdied the 34th, eagled the 35th to go 1 up and halved the 36th

Forever Grateful

By Tom Watson

On a cool and damp late Sunday afternoon in June of 1974, I was sitting with my friend and fellow golfer, John Mahaffey, in the upper locker room of Winged Foot Golf Club, after shooting a 79 to lose to Hale Irwin in the final round of the U.S. Open. John was trying to cheer me up when something unexpected occurred that was to add a dimension to my life for which I will be forever grateful. Into the room walked Byron Nelson, who had just finished his ABC commentary. John and I stopped our conversation and greeted Byron with the respect he engenders in everyone who ever meets him.

After saying his hellos, he turned to me with, "Tom, could I have five minutes of your time?" I had met Byron just once before, so this request was quite surprising. I shook off my despair, and we walked to an empty row of lockers.

It was a conversation that changed my game and, in many ways, my life.

When I turned professional in 1971, I didn't know what to expect from the PGA Tour, so I asked some of the best sources I knew: the local Kansas City golf professionals. When I played with them on their Monday day off, my questions ranged from how to travel to what the courses were like. But everyone I asked always answered the most crucial question—What one thing should I do to make myself a success—the same way. They all said, "Observe and play with the best players."

It was a logical answer to me because I had always watched the great swings of Stan Thirsk, Duke Gibson, and, of course, my father and his friends, who were all accomplished amateurs. All the best golfers' swings are different, from their rhythm to their fundamentals. So I observed as much as I could, everywhere I could.

It didn't take me long to see that studying the strong golfers in a generation naturally led to looking back at their predecessors, the ones they'd observed. For example, leading the way for players such as Arnold Palmer and Jack Nicklaus had been the great triumvirate of the 1940s and '50s: Ben Hogan, Sam Snead and Byron Nelson.

I first heard about Byron Nelson from my father, who taught me not only how to play the game, but also its history. He was an avid admirer of Bobby Jones and Sam Snead, but whenever the "greats" were discussed, he never failed to mention Byron and his incredible streak in 1945 of 11 wins in a row. My father talked about Byron's pronounced "dip" in his swing; many years later, I learned that dip was the reason Byron hit the ball as straight as any golfer who ever played the game. Byron retired in 1946 when he decided that ranching offered more to life for him and his wife Louise than traveling in a sedan following the sun. Raising cattle and chickens became his work, but golf was still in his

◄

Tom Watson waits on the first tee at the 1997 Masters as Byron looks on.

blood. He remained active, playing an odd tournament here and there — and still winning here and there.

Then Arnold Palmer and televised golf happened on the scene at the same time, and golf's popularity soared. Television needed experts who could explain the situations viewers were seeing, as well as analyze the varied golf swings of the

> *"I have seen Byron swing the golf club thousands of times during our lessons, and I have to admit I would never have had a chance to win if I had played him in his prime."*

professionals that so many amateurs and fans were seeing for the first time. ABC Television hired Byron Nelson to be its expert analyst. Through television, the tall legend with the Texas drawl became famous all over again, this time to a whole new generation.

It was after he had finished commentating on the 1974 U.S. Open to viewers that he gave me my first lesson. In his straightforward but self-effacing manner, Byron talked first about my play on the previous day, when I had taken the third-round lead with a 69. Then he discussed the difference he saw in my swing in the just-completed final round. He explained to me that the leg action he observed in my swing on Saturday was not the same as it was on Sunday. Quite simply, my leg action was out of sync with the swing of my arms on Sunday where it was well synchronized during my good play on Saturday. At the end of his gentle, spirit-raising analysis, he made an offer that would alter the course of my career. He invited me to come to his Texas home, Fairway Ranch, to spend some time eating Louise's great cooking. He also suggested that during the visit he would like to help me with my golf swing.

In the autumn of 1976, after a year of poor play, I took Byron up on his offer and went down to Roanoke to visit the Nelsons and to work on my golf game. The warmth of their home was matched by their humility. Louise's cooking was superb. And Byron's knowledge about the golf swing was as fundamental as it was unlimited.

From there my career truly jumped to the next level. In 1977, I won back-to-back tournaments early on and added both the Masters and the British Open to end up the leading money winner and PGA Player of the Year. I owe Byron a great deal of credit for my success that year and the years following.

My first outing with Byron was a lesson in simplicity. He showed me how to swing by swinging his own club in the perfect path — his way. I still to this day marvel at the way he swings the club. A study in high-speed photography conducted at the field house of Purdue University showed that Byron's clubhead through impact remained facing the target considerably longer than Hogan's, Snead's or Jimmy Demaret's, golfers considered to have the best swings of their time.

Tom Watson at the 1974 U.S. Open at Winged Foot.

Byron's swing featured little of the clubhead rotation the other top players had. His clubhead was square through the impact area for an unbelievable 11 inches or so. In other words, his clubhead was absolutely square to the intended flight of the ball for about six inches behind the ball and about the same through it! His legs literally carried the clubface through impact and his leg action prevented the clubface from rotating or turning over.

Just before the Nelson Classic at Preston Trail many years ago, during a clinic for young golfers, I asked Byron to hit his driver—not an unusual request, except to make it more challenging for a man of his talent, I stipulated that he must hit the golf balls off the ground. In this day and age, hitting a metal driver off the ground is fairly easy. Back then, however, there were only wooden drivers that required extraordinary skill to loft the ball into the air. First, I asked him to hit a hook, which is the toughest, then a fade, and, finally, the straight ball. He hit every one perfectly, much to the joy of all the kids, their parents and especially me.

I have seen Byron swing the golf club thousands of times during our lessons, and I have to admit in writing that I would never have had a chance to win if I had played him in his prime. I can honestly say that I have never seen him hit what I consider a wild shot! Duck hooks and push slices were just not in his repertoire of shots. During our practice sessions, I have often needled him when he was hitting balls about hitting a pull hook or a wicked slice—but for him, it was only a slight pull or push at the worst.

It's probably safe to say that everyone who ever worked with Byron came away a better golfer. Ken Venturi, whom I consider to have been one of the best strikers of the ball, worked in his early years with Byron and attests to his mentor's abilities, not only as a player, but as a teacher as well. Not every great player is a great teacher. Byron Nelson was doubly gifted.

He showed me a myriad of technical things that stuck with me. Technically, he asked me to move my lower body more in my takeaway. But I believe that his secret had more to do with my mind than my golf swing. The most important thing Byron had to share was his attitude.

Tom Watson has won the Byron Nelson Classic four times, including three in a row (1978-80).

Here's an example. In 1945, he said, he kept one thought uppermost in his mind: "I'm going to concentrate on every shot this year." He said that he would remind himself, "I'm not going to hit too quickly without having an idea firmly in my mind of what I'm going to do." Byron played very fast, like me. One of the reasons he enjoyed coaching me, he used to say, was that I played without delay. But that year, Byron played one shot at a time. And it was his great year. He finished in the top three in 26 out of 30 tournaments and in the top five in 28 out of 30, a record still unmatched and probably set as much by attitude as play. (The other two finishes were ties for sixth and ninth.)

He brought that same kind of attitude to his teaching. He always took a positive outlook about the way I was hitting, even when I wasn't hitting very well. He never said, "Watson, you're not swinging well." Instead, he'd say something like, "I've never seen you hit the ball so well." He wasn't patronizing. He was trying to make me feel I was swinging better than I was physically hitting the ball. By always thinking positively and reinforcing my confidence, even when I was swinging poorly, he made me play better.

That kind of thinking is important to succeeding not only in golf but also in life. Since I first went to Roanoke in 1976, those lessons have helped me on and off the course. Byron Nelson has been a father figure to me: a great teacher and a great friend.

A. Ravielli

Pioneering Legacy

By Nick Seitz

Whoever said records are made to be broken did not stop to consider John Byron Nelson, Jr. whose records for most victories and lowest scoring average in a season will last as long as calendars list 12 months and golf is played, or longer. So monumental were his 1945 feats, they assume almost mythical proportions, their glare blinding us, like the high-beam headlights of an oncoming truck, to Nelson's many other pioneering achievements.

Off the course, this commanding Currier & Ives figure demonstrated the same kind of innovative, fecund imagination that made him a legendary golfer. You could even say the courtly Nelson was a homespun genius of sorts without stretching the point—a pioneer without peer in his chosen field.

He is known as the father of the modern golf swing—a primary influence on the best teachers and players of subsequent generations, even if many of them lack the sense of history to realize it. Nelson became the first superstar to serve as a mentor to promising young pros. He is the first and only pro golfer for whom a PGA Tour event is named: the GTE Byron Nelson Classic in the Dallas area. He was the first pro to do live television golf commentary regularly.

Let us continue to count the ways Nelson built a legacy like no other in the game. He inspired the design of the golf shoe and golf umbrella as we know them today. And, oh yes, the first nursery on tour was his idea: a man with no children of his own concerned with child care, a concept ahead of his time.

Necessity is the mother of invention, and also its father and Dutch uncle. Where he saw a need, the unassuming Nelson quietly but firmly addressed it. A man of little formal schooling, he had an affinity for numbers and a shrewd head for business, his instincts honed by years of running golf shops as a club pro in the off-season, before the tour became a profitable full-time calling for its practitioners. Always that agile imagination was ready to rise to a stimulus.

The evolution of the swing without Nelson would be like the evolution of music without Beethoven. He was the crucial watershed at the crossroads of the swing's transition from classical to modern, the first man to build a swing for steel shafts—a swing that itself suggested the tautness and strength of steel.

Jack Nicklaus won the Byron Nelson Golf Classic in 1970 and 1971.

Nelson minimized and solidified his swing so it would repeat under the fiercest pressure, and the finished product amounted to a paradigm shift, as the scientists would put it. A model of streamlined efficiency, his modern action featured (in tech talk) a one-piece takeaway, upright plane, left-side control and flex-kneed leg drive, all blended at a smooth, unforced pace. It was the antithesis of the elegantly long and flippy swing that had worked with the flexible wooden shafts until about 1930.

> "*Ah, consistency. It became Nelson's hallmark, his proudest accomplishment. He distilled the swing to its essence the way Hemingway distilled the language...*"

The bigger, 1.68-inch ball was coming into play at about the same time, and Nelson's rebuilt swing proved best for striking it crisply. He moved the clubhead along the target line longer at takeaway and through impact, holding the clubface square to its path, and accuracy was the inevitable consequence. "The only time Byron left the fairway," Jackie Burke, Jr. once said, "was to visit the bushes."

Nelson never obsessed about distance. He normally made only a three-quarter swing with a driver, and everybody else looked loose by comparison. The courses were shorter, if poorly conditioned, and he could hit it far enough to dominate. "Nelson hit his fairway woods just as far as he hit his driver," remembers Paul Runyan. "Even though he wasn't terribly long, he was a great driver. He could turn the ball in either direction, and he could do one thing even Nicklaus couldn't do: he could keep the ball down into the wind."

I asked Nelson about his fatherhood of the modern swing.

"I get credit for that because I started using the feet and legs to get more freedom down below," he said in his metallic Texas twang, gesturing with freckled, steam-shovel hands, whose sensitivity he considered his greatest gift. "Before, with hickory shafts, you had to roll the club open on the backswing, then roll it closed on the downswing and hit against a stiff leg. It was hard to be consistent. So I started using my lower body more to keep the clubface square."

How would he contrast his swing with the swings he sees on tour today?

"My backswing wasn't nearly as long as what you see now. I never cocked my wrists at the top of the swing at all. I led my downswing with my feet and legs and had a downcock with my wrists on the downswing. The good players today distribute their weight and use the lower body the way I did, but they have lengthened their backswings to parallel or even beyond. The timing looks a little slower and smoother, and they've gained distance. I drove the ball 254 yards on average. They drive it 20 to 25 yards farther than that. The shafts and ball are a little better, but they've lengthened the swing dramatically."

BYRON NELSON

Ben Hogan and Paul Runyan look over Byron's scorecard at Augusta in the early 1940s.

Nelson's influence on teaching was seminal, says David Leadbetter, one of today's top teachers: "He was the major influence on the modern swing and its teaching because he was the transition swinger from hickory to steel, more so than Bobby Jones. Until Nelson, the swing was very much a hands-and-arms motion. He started to use his legs more to keep the ball down, keep his hands quieter through the ball."

Bob Toski, the first superstar teacher, believes Nelson's effect on modern teaching was profound.

Nelson in action in the '40s.

"I never heard him talk about 'coil' or 'resistance with the lower body' the way you hear so many teachers talk today. Those approaches take away motion—they're too mechanical. You lose a sense of rhythm, and add stress. The average golfer needs less resistance and stress, not more."

The expressive Toski all but raves about Nelson's swing. "He created power with his lower-body action—he had so much knee flex he almost genuflected—and he had unbelievably quick hand action through impact. It's a great way to play if you're strong enough. The real test of a swing is hitting a driver off a tight fairway. At Cypress Point one time, I saw Byron hit 20 drivers off the ground practicing, and the trajectory never varied. I've never seen that before or since. Those huge hands could trap a ball against the ground with a 2-iron and make it hold a 10-foot trajectory for 200 yards. Unbelievable!"

Runyan makes the point that Nelson was one of a precious few players he's seen who contacted the ball at the very bottom of the swing arc, precisely and cleanly and solidly, which is why he was so wondrously effective with his fairway woods and longer irons. Everyone else either "pinched" the ball and took a meaty divot or hit up on it slightly. Nelson caught it flush, as they say, and he did so almost every time he swung in the mid-1940s. He may have taken the best divots in history—that is to say, virtually no divots at all. "I just skimmed the turf," he says.

Byron, the reigning U.S. Open champ, met Henry Picard in the final of the 1939 PGA Championship. Byron lost 1 down on the 37th hole.

Nelson tells a story of a clinic he staged at Los Angeles Country Club. The practice range was muddy, and he convinced tournament officials to let him hit from the turf in the front of the first tee box, promising he wouldn't damage it. After he was finished, you could barely tell he'd been there.

"I learned to play in the wind on firm turf, and I always felt I could make as good contact off concrete as off grass," Nelson says. "Clover took over a lot of fairways we played back then, but I never hit flyers because I just kinda clipped the ball."

Nelson did not develop the modern swing without a painful period of trial and error and travail, a long battle with the hated shanks included. In working his lower body more vigorously on the downswing, he at first allowed his head to move too much also, inviting shanks. "It got so bad I would shank for weeks," he remembered. "Eventually I deter-

"Winners are different. They have an inner drive and are willing to give whatever it takes to win. It's a discipline a lot of people are not willing to put on themselves."

mined that if I would hit out from under my head, keeping the head back while my lower body shifted past it, I wouldn't shank. A steady head is the secret to balance, and keeping my head still was the change that let everything begin to fall into place."

Nelson always has had a knack for fresh, vivid phraseology to convey and leaven his swing keys, as the splendid book he wrote with Larry Dennis in 1976, *"Shape Your Swing the Modern Way,"* amply shows. "Freedom down below keeps the head still." "If you swing harder, stand closer." "Hang on with the left hand for consistency."

Ah, consistency. It became Nelson's hallmark, his proudest accomplishment. He distilled the swing to its essence the way Hemingway distilled the language, and once he mastered his modern method he was almost unbeatable, able to do anything with the ball but mis-hit it. He aspired to be a golfing automaton—"You practice so the body can become a repetitive machine"—and it is no coincidence that the mechanical golfer the U.S. Golf Association uses for testing is based on Nelson's action, and is called "Iron Byron."

Byron signing copies of his book, *Winning Golf,* in Portland in late 1946.

Bob Bush was working for True Temper, the shaft company, when the robotic golfer was born in 1964. He says, "We found from studying high-speed movies and other materials that Byron's swing represented the most efficient use of energy of any tour players of that time. All swings have some wasted energy, but his had the least. It was astonishing that in helping us with the prototype he was just about as accurate and repeating as the machine itself."

Once his contained swing was grooved to this level of reliability, Nelson practiced little. Golf historian Bill Inglish remembers that his pre-round warmup typically consisted of a half-dozen to a dozen shots, as Nelson all but stopped hitting balls and experimenting, perhaps one reason he was able to withstand the pressures of his 1945 season so well. "I didn't practice much once I had formed my swing," he said in 1996 at the PGA Teaching Summit where he was a featured guest. "Certainly not as much as Ben Hogan. He poked fun at me once on a radio show when he told the announcer I was lazy. But I could go three weeks without touching a club and it wouldn't affect me at all. Once you find something in your swing that works and is fundamentally sound, stay with it. If your game goes sour, resist the temptation to fool with that fundamental. For the average golfer, experimenting is death."

Nelson's reputation as a teacher began to build soon after he left the tour. He has worked with, among others, Harvie Ward, Frank Stranahan, Tony Lema, Bobby Nichols, and, most notably, Tom Watson and Ken Venturi. I have watched him help Watson, and

Harvie Ward, one of Byron's early pupils.

his approach was casually intent, if somewhat different. Much of the time he would study the player from the rear, to check his balance and weight shift. Balance was very big in Nelson's thinking. He would call for different shot shapes as Watson went through the bag, asking that a 5-iron be hit high from left to right, then, on the next shot, low from right to left. Never did he seem to overcoach.

Much of Nelson's mentoring has consisted of light doses of low-key psychology; he serves as a patiently authoritative sounding board about top-level competition. So mild-mannered is Nelson, who easily could be mistaken for a Sunday school teacher every day of the week, his attitude toward winning has always been undervalued. Says Runyan, an astute student of professional golf for 75 years, "I rank him the No. 1 competitor of all. He has the fiercest competitive disposition I've ever known. At the Masters one time he came into the locker room so mad he was almost apoplectic. I thought he must have shot 80. I asked him what he'd shot, and he said 66. He said if he'd had me putting for him he'd have broken 60. It turned out he hit every green, in four *under* regulation, which was unheard of, and had 34 putts on those tricky greens. He was a brilliant putter. Once he stopped shanking, he was magnificent in every category of play. But he was so intense he retired early."

Nelson says, "Winners are different. They have an inner drive and are willing to give whatever it takes to win. It's a discipline a lot of people are not willing to put on themselves. It takes a different way of thinking and a lot of energy. It makes a different demand on you to win tournaments than to just go out to win money."

For a decade it was traditional for Nelson the mentor to be paired with the leader the last day of the Masters, an honor bestowed on him by Bobby Jones. The practice ended in 1956 because Venturi was leading, and tournament officials feared he might gain an unfair advantage being paired with his coach. Venturi shot 80 the final day, letting Jackie Burke make up eight strokes to win, and we can only speculate how much Nelson, who

Two-time PGA champion and short-game wizard Paul Runyan considers Byron to be the fiercest competitor of all time as well as a brilliant putter.

played with seven Masters winners in his honorary role, might have stabilized the young amateur.

Nelson would amaze his pupils like Venturi by telling them that there was no such thing as a touring caddie in his day because the players couldn't afford them. "We were just trying to get to the next town. I'd be in the red, taking my winnings against my expenses." Nelson, a meticulous recordkeeper and diarist about his golf travels and competition, can show you the figures.

The "Umbrella Man." To supplement his income

Byron with pupil Ken Venturi at the Masters in 1965. Ken was the reigning U.S. Open Champion.

on tour, Nelson called on customers for the Haas-Jordan Company, still a leading manufacturer of the golf umbrellas he inspired. "In 1946 I came home to rest the week of the tournament in Richmond, California," Nelson says, "and when I was asked why I wasn't playing I said I needed to sell some umbrellas. It got passed along, and I became known as the 'Umbrella Man'."

Haas-Jordan was first known for women's umbrellas. Nelson was hired as the club pro at Inverness in Toledo by Cloyd Haas, the head of the company, and sold Haas on the concept for the modern golf umbrella.

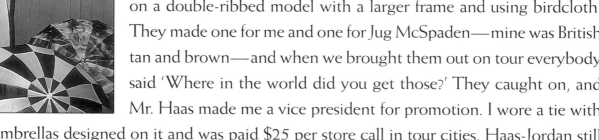

COURTESY HAAS-JORDAN

Byron Nelson, the "Umbrella Man."

Nelson says, "We were having dinner at his house one night, and I told him we had terrible umbrellas on tour. They were weak-framed, blew inside out in the wind, and let water through. I said if he could make such a good lady's umbrella, he ought to make a good umbrella for golf, larger with a stronger frame and waterproof material. We went to the plant in New Jersey the next week and decided on a double-ribbed model with a larger frame and using birdcloth. They made one for me and one for Jug McSpaden—mine was British tan and brown—and when we brought them out on tour everybody said 'Where in the world did you get those?' They caught on, and Mr. Haas made me a vice president for promotion. I wore a tie with umbrellas designed on it and was paid $25 per store call in tour cities. Haas-Jordan still makes the umbrellas for the Ryder Cup team and others."

Invention breeds invention, it is said. Nelson provoked Haas-Jordan into the golf-umbrella business, and he and McSpaden pushed Foot-Joy into the golf shoe business, starting in 1938. They were at Pinehurst for the North and South tournament, talking to Miles Baker, a saleman for Field and Flint which made the Foot-Joy line. The two players were complaining about the flimsiness of their golf shoes. "The soles were so thin you could feel the spikes almost right through the leather," Nelson recalled in his autobiography, "and when we had to play on a wet course, the shoes wouldn't hold up at all."

The Gold Dust Twins, as Nelson and Mc-Spaden were known, challenged Baker to come up with a better golf shoe: thicker soled and broader across the ball of the foot. Not much later, the two pros went to the Foot-Joy factory near Boston, where special shoe lasts were made for them, then

ASSOCIATED PRESS

The Gold Dust Twins: Byron and Jug at the Miami Four-Ball in 1946. Note their Foot-Joy shoes which they were largely responsible for developing.

custom shoes, Nelson's in his favorite colors of British tan and brown with wingtips. The rest of the tour was envious, and Foot-Joy was launched as a force in golf. "They paid us a 25-cent royalty per pair for quite a few years," said Nelson.

When he got the Inverness job in 1940, one of the first things Nelson did was stock up on shoes to sell the members. His friend Miles Baker helped him select 84 pairs of Foot-Joys, both street and golf shoes. "He told me I was really the first pro to do this,"

Nelson said. "Most pros would have sample pairs of different styles, but the members had to order them and wait several weeks to get them. My stock covered all the styles in just about all the sizes, which made it very convenient to sell the shoes on the spot." The shrewd head for business was on the high setting once again.

Nelson came too early to share in the endorsements bonanza his successors take for granted. A big deal for him was the umbrella or shoe deal or his contract with Wheaties that provided mostly free cereal.

Now in his 80s, Nelson no longer wears spiked shoes to play occasional nine-hole rounds, having avidly converted in recent years to the new spikeless version. "I wouldn't play without 'em," he says enthusiastically. "They're comfortable and great for me because I have a little trouble picking up my feet since I had hip surgery. And at home you don't have to change shoes back and forth."

Would he wear them if he were competing today?

"I think so. I don't find that I slip any more on slopes or wet walkways than I did with the old spikes."

To golf followers in the '60s and '70s, Nelson was better known as a pioneering television commentator than a pioneering anything else. He began that career at the Masters, where Frank Chirkinian hired him for CBS at the instigation of tournament major domo Clifford Roberts. Compulsively worried about possible vulgarization of the classic event, Roberts figured Nelson could avoid talking about money, the size of the crowds and other common media topics Roberts deemed no-nos.

Byron in the pro shop with Ed Sullivan.

Nelson worked with Chris Schenkel, and it was the start of a long partnership and friendship. In 1963, Nelson went on to sign with ABC, which was making golf a cornerstone of its sports programming, and Schenkel followed a year later. Nelson fondly remembers Schenkel as a most helpful mentor, Byron's usual role in life, and the fastest golfer he's ever played with. He remembers Roone Arledge, the reclusive brains behind ABC Sports and later ABC News, as a pest about Nelson's Texas expressions and probably the slowest golfer he's ever played with. Schenkel counseled Nelson to ignore Arledge and be himself on the air, and Nelson did, capitulating only on his pronunciation of Bermuda ("Bermooda" in Texan).

Nelson was responsible for the introduction of the plexiglass screen in front of golf announcers because his voice inevitably carried to the green when players were putting. He remembers Billy Casper thanking him for his audible read of a birdie putt that Casper sank on 18 in the 1964 World Series of Golf.

The most exciting shot he saw doing TV was Jack Nicklaus' 1-iron on the 17th hole at Pebble Beach the last day of the 1972 U.S. Open. Piercing a bitter wind, the ball grazed the bottom of the flagstick and dropped a few inches from the hole to assure victory.

The 1976 U.S. Open that Jerry Pate won with his own 24-karat iron shot was Nelson's final telecast. ABC was changing directions with its coverage, relying more on a "foot soldier" concept to supplement an anchor who would do diagrams and overviews, and Nelson wasn't comfortable with it. Also he had wearied of the travel at age 64. So he told Arledge and producer Chuck Howard he thought that it was a good time to leave, and they accepted his decision without undue protest.

Howard said before his death in 1996, "Byron had that Texas folksiness, and he was never critical of the players, but he won people over with his sincerity and insight. Remember he was the first to do it regularly, so there were no precedents. He wasn't Johnny Miller or Gary McCord, but he paved the way for them."

> "*Says [Corey] Pavin, 'Byron's a beautiful person. He's my hero. I've had a fairly decent career, and won 11 times on tour. He won 11 in a row! He's the first teacher who said something good about my swing.'*"

Howard remembered that in 1967 Nelson analyzed Baltusrol for a U.S. Open preview show and predicted a record winning score of 275. That's the score Nicklaus shot a couple of weeks later.

My recollection of those years when Nelson and Schenkel established themselves as the first famous golf announcing team is that Schenkel, consummate professional broadcaster that he is, failed to fulfill the rabid golfer-viewer's desire for inside knowledge by drawing out his expert colleague. In person, Nelson was forthrightly stimulating; on air he seldom generated the verbal momentum to make a point as fully as he might have. "Is that how you did it back in '45, pro?" was a standard Schenkel setup, and a joke of the day went that Nelson popularized the expression "That's right, Chris."

But of Schenkel, to whom he has remained close, Nelson offers only the most laudatory praise. Lord Byron is a man's gentleman who does not smoke, drink, swear, watch X-rated videos or speak ill of his fellow man. He and Schenkel dutifully reported what was happening and never offended anyone, and that isn't the worst testimonial in the cutthroat world of television.

Nelson's happiest hours in the medium came when he was covering his own tournament, the former Dallas Open that took on his name 30 years ago. Owing to the dedicated efforts of Nelson and the Salesmanship Club of Dallas, a co-sponsoring civic organization, the tournament raises more money for charity than any other. The money goes to a children's rehabilitation program that includes summer camps and a plethora of other activities in the area. If the tour sometimes braggeth too much about its charitable contributions that justify its tax-exempt status, Nelson's tournament is the most impressive example of how at least some tournaments deserve their altruistic reputation.

Byron along with Chris Schenkel were the featured commentators on ABC's pioneering golf telecasts in the 1960s.

The Nelson purse has kept pace with the biggest on tour, and was to go to $2 million in 1998. When Nelson won the Texas Victory Open in Dallas in 1944, the forerunner of his tournament, the total purse was $10,000...Nelson's share $2,000.

If he resents the rampant riches on today's tour and being born 50 years too soon, he conceals it well. "What I won was a lot of money to me at the time, and I don't know what I would want to do that I haven't been fortunate enough to do," he told me a few years ago. "Ben Hogan has said that the boys today don't enjoy the game as much as we did, which is quite a statement coming from a man as serious about his golf as Ben always has been, and I believe there's something to that."

Nelson still attends the tour sponsors' meetings, bringing a realistic viewpoint on the escalating purses. "I told them a few years back we were headed for million-dollar purses, and they hooted at me," he says today. "I tell 'em now I don't know how high they might go—maybe to 10 before long. Nobody hoots."

The recruiting competition for top players has escalated along with the purses, but Nelson holds his own with a soft-sell approach. When a pro wins a tournament he gets a cordial congratulatory note from Nelson, but never asking him to play in the Dallas event. Phil Mickelson wasn't planning to play in the 1996 Nelson Classic, but he changed his mind after getting a note from its namesake. He won the tournament.

Every Sunday finisher at Nelson's event gets, in addition to his paycheck, a warm handshake and thank-you from the legend himself. Some stars, like Watson and Corey Pavin, hold Nelson in such high esteem there is never any doubt they will enter. Watson, who visited Nelson's first wife numerous times during her last illness, has won it four times, the most of anyone, and has made major, quiet contributions to the Salesmanship Club. Said Pavin in 1997, "Byron's a beautiful person. He's my hero. I've had a fairly decent career, and won 11 times on tour. He won 11 in a row! He's the first teacher who said something good about my swing."

The Salesmanship Club of Dallas, the sponsor of the GTE Byron Nelson Classic, provides assistance and guidance to troubled youth.

Nelson says, "I go with our committee to The Players Championship, and that's the first place I see the boys—the only official place. Most of 'em, as soon as they see me, will say 'I'm comin', I'm comin.' During the year I'll see them at the Masters where I'm an honorary starter and usually at the U.S. Open and the PGA and the Colonial next door, and I'll be somewhere like LaCosta getting or presenting an award and not just promoting our event."

The No. 1 attraction of the era is Tiger Woods, and Nelson can find no fault with the young man's swing or attitude. "I knew him for five years before he came on the tour," he says, "and I've been a fan for a long time. I went out and watched him in Bel-Air when he was a junior player, and he won a junior tournament here. He played in our tournament as an amateur. His biggest challenge will be sorting out his opportunities. His distance—his length—I don't understand."

Woods will win 13 to 20 major championships, depending on which overexcited expert you listen to. No one is predicting he'll have a year like 1945, though. There won't be another one like that, or another man who would carry the records as nobly and modestly as the pioneering Byron Nelson.

Byron rides one of the early golf carts at the Colonial Tournament in Fort Worth.

Lord Byron: A Local Angle

So I'm sitting here staring the millennium in the teeth, and I'm thinking that one of the things I definitely plan to carry into the dreaded 21st century, along with my grandmother's recipe for chicken and dumplings, is the memory of watching Byron Nelson play golf at his peak.

In all of the years that have passed since then, I can't think of anything else in the realm of art that would compare with it. Oh, well, maybe the Sistine Chapel. Perhaps a few bars of Tchaikovsky. Certainly a plate of that chicken and dumplings.

I don't know how many fans are still around who had the pleasure of seeing Nelson strike the golf ball when he was "Lord Byron Nelson, golf's mechanical man." Not too many sportswriters, I dare say.

Most of the sportswriters of Byron's decade have gone on to the big hospitality tent in the sky, and no offense but several of those I know today tend to wear shorts, sneakers, drink diet sodas and have to go to the Internet to determine whether 1945 was the era of Napoleon or the Crusades.

I was a junior in high school in '45, and only a sportswriter if you want to count *The Paschal Pantherette*, and...wait a second.

You know what? I think I should start with the first time I ever saw Byron Nelson, or any other bigtime pro.

Cut to June 4, 1941, Colonial Country Club, Fort Worth, Texas. Day before the start of the U.S. Open, the first to be held west of the Mississippi.

I'm only 11 years old. But I'm out there, as I would be for the whole championship. Me in my little green-and-white striped slipover polo shirt, as they were known in those days, a pair of little brown moccasins on my feet and a big ticket tied on my belt. What the well-dressed preteen would wear to a U.S. Open.

I'd been set loose at Colonial by a dad, an uncle and an older cousin who had told me to go find Byron Nelson and Ben Hogan, have a nice day.

"Nelson and Hogan are the two greatest golfers in the world," the uncle said, adding proudly, "and they're from Fort Worth, just like you."

My first discovery involved haberdashery. Most of the bigtime pros were wearing beltless slacks, I noted, slightly wide-eyed. Such fashion for gentlemen hadn't arrived in my neighborhood at the time.

But this was nothing compared to the sight of Colonial's bent greens, which were the first ever grown in the Southwest, I would later learn.

To a kid who had never seen a putting surface that wasn't made out of Bermuda, sand,

By Dan Jenkins

◀
Byron in action.

TEMPLE UNIVERSITY ARCHIVES/ASSOCIATED PRESS

Major League Competition

Quaker Ridge Golf Club
Scarsdale, New York
May 21-23, 1936

After respectable finishes in the 1935 and 1936 Masters, Byron won his first major event, the 1936 Metropolitan Open. The host club was the Quaker Ridge Golf Club in Scarsdale, New York—just across the street from its younger Tillinghast sibling Winged Foot.

With scores of 71-69-72-71 for a 283 total, Byron outlasted a fine field that included Denny Shute, Horton Smith, Vic Ghezzi and Gene Sarazen, and won his first truly big tournament.

1936 MET OPEN		
1. Byron Nelson	71 – 69 – 72 – 71 – 283
2. Craig Wood	71 – 70 – 71 – 73 – 285
3. Paul Runyan	71 – 67 – 73 – 75 – 286
4. Henry Picard	70 – 72 – 74 – 73 – 289
5. Willie Macfarlane	72 – 71 – 75 – 75 – 293

Top: Given an assistant pro's income, all Byron could afford for lunch during the tournament was a hot dog and a Coke.

Small photo, far right: Byron pitches out of trouble.

Large photo: Nelson putts for birdie on the par-three ninth.

The Leader for the First Two Rounds

yron continued his fine play in big tournaments posting a first-round score of six-under-par 66 to set the lead on the opening day. Byron played magnificently: four birdies on the front nine, six one-putt greens overall and reaching the uphill par-five eighth hole in two. It was quite a performance for the up-and-coming 25-year-old.

In the second round Byron shot an even-par 72 but retained the lead by three strokes over Ralph Guldahl and Ed Dudley. In the third round, Guldahl posted a superb 68 to pick up seven shots on Byron, as he recorded a 75 for third spot going into Sunday's final round, just behind Ed Dudley one stroke ahead.

TEMPLE UNIVERSITY ARCHIVES/ACME

Above: Byron posts a first-round leading 66. Note how the scorekeeper has misspelled his first name.

Right: With Johnny Revolta (second from left) waiting to tee off, Byron drives from the first tee in the 1937 Masters. Seated at the starter's table is golf impresario Fred Corcoran (at right) with Cliff Roberts standing behind him.

Left: Byron lines up another putt on the slick Augusta greens.

Above: A happy winner.

Big Doings in the Fourth Round!

$\mathcal{T}$he fourth round was a humdinger! With Guldahl playing with Ky Laffoon three groups ahead, both Guldahl and Byron—playing with veteran Wiffy Cox—made the turn in a two-over 38.

But it was on the back that the pyrotechnics—and golf history—occurred.

With seven holes to play, Byron was still four shots down, the same margin as when he started the day. As Guldahl made a double-bogey five on the treacherous 12th and a bogey six on the 13th, (both times catching the water), Byron birdied the 12th and eagled the 13th—incredibly picking up six shots in just two holes!

Although Guldahl birdied the 15th to draw closer, he also bogeyed the 17th as Byron parred in for the two-shot victory.

This stretch of holes on Augusta's back nine—the 11th, 12th and 13th, so aptly named "Amen Corner" by Herbert Warren Wind—had proved to be the a turning point in this fourth playing of the Masters, just as it would for decades to come.

Right: Byron with runner-up Ralph Guldahl.

The First Augusta Win

Byron Nelson, age 25, had won his first Masters by two strokes over Ralph Guldahl, three strokes over the home professional Ed Dudley and by four strokes over "Light Horse" Harry Cooper. Byron collected his winner's check of $1,500 from Grantland Rice, the legendary sports writer and editor of *The American Golfer* magazine and a founding member of the Augusta National Golf Club.

1937 MASTERS	
1. Byron Nelson	66 – 72 – 75 – 70 – 283
2. Ralph Guldahl	69 – 72 – 68 – 76 – 285
3. Ed Dudley	70 – 71 – 71 – 74 – 286
4. Harry Cooper	73 – 69 – 71 – 74 – 287
5. Ky Laffoon	73 – 70 – 74 – 73 – 290

Above: The first four Masters Tournament winners: Gene Sarazen, Horton Smith, Byron and Henry Picard.

Left: Byron receives his first-place check for $1,500 from Grantland Rice as Ralph Guldahl (left) and Ed Dudley look on.

Ryder Cup Rookie

Southport and Ainsdale Golf Club
Southport, England
June 29-30, 1937

*W*ith the winds of war beginning to be heard across Europe, the American Ryder Cup Team traveled to Great Britain to do battle with the British team for the sixth playing of the biennial Ryder Cup Matches at the Southport and Ainsdale Golf Club in Southport, England.

The American Team, captained by the flamboyant five-time PGA Champion Walter Hagen, consisted of Sam Snead, 1937 U.S. Open Champion Ralph Guldahl, Ed Dudley, Johnny Revolta, 1937 Masters Tournament winner Byron Nelson, 1937 PGA Champion Denny Shute, Henry Picard, Horton Smith, Tony Manero and Gene Sarazen.

Six members of the American side were chosen on the basis of performance during the preceding two years while the remaining were added after performance in the U.S. Open. The British Team was chosen by a selection committee.

Above: Members of the American and English Ryder Cup teams in a practice session just before the beginning of the Matches at Southport. (Left to right) Ed Dudley, Denny Shute, Henry Cotton, Alf Padgham and Byron enjoy a light moment.

Left: Sir Phillip Sassoon hosted a party for the 1937 Ryder Cup teams at his home in London.

Inset: Denny and Potsy Shute with the Nelsons on the ship en route to the Ryder Cup.

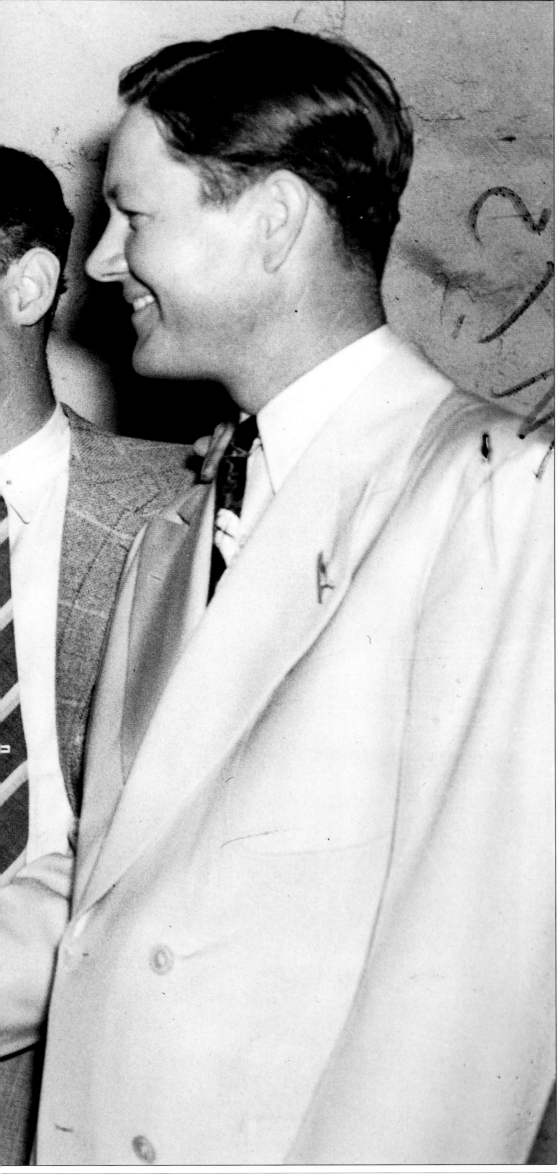

The First Playoff

O ver the first nine holes, the playoff quickly settled into a match between Nelson and Wood as they both posted one-under-par 33s; Denny Shute was three back at 37. All even through the 16th hole, Wood parred as Byron bogeyed and Shute also bogeyed, to effectively put himself out of the running. Byron, with a clutch birdie 4 on 18 to Wood's par 5, tied with Wood at 68, as Shute was eliminated with a seven-over-par 76.

THE FIRST PLAYOFF

HOLE	1	2	3	4	5	6	7	8	9	Out
PAR	4	3	4	4	4	4	3	4	4	34
NELSON	4	3	4	4	5	4	2	4	3	33
WOOD	4	3	4	4	4	3	3	4	4	33
SHUTE	4	4	4	4	4	5	3	4	5	37

HOLE	10	11	12	13	14	15	16	17	18	In
PAR	4	3	4	3	4	4	4	4	5	35
NELSON	4	4	3	4	4	4	3	5	4	35
WOOD	5	3	4	3	4	4	3	4	5	35
SHUTE	4	3	4	4	4	4	4	5	7	39

NELSON	33–35	68
WOOD	33–35	68
SHUTE	37–39	76

Above: Byron with Ed Dudley shortly before teeing off for the 1939 U.S. Open Championship over the Spring Mill Course.

Left: 1938 U.S. Open Champion Ralph Guldahl symbolically passes the Open trophy to the three participants in the playoff.

Left: Byron and Craig Wood tied with 68s to force a second 18-hole playoff.

The Second Playoff

*W*ith a birdie at the par-four third and an eagle on the par-four fourth (a full one-iron from the fairway!), Byron took a four-stroke lead. Never relinquishing his edge the rest of the day, Byron shot a one-over 33-37-70 with an eagle, two birdies and five bogeys over the tough 6,786-yard par-69 layout to Wood's 36-37-73 (three birdies, eight bogeys) for the National Championship.

In 1939 the Rules of Golf required that the pin be either attended or taken out if you were within 60 feet.

THE SECOND PLAYOFF									
HOLE	1	2	3	4	5	6	7	8	9	**Out**
PAR	4	3	4	4	4	4	3	4	4	34
NELSON	4	3	3	2	5	5	3	4	4	33
WOOD	5	2	5	4	4	4	3	4	5	36
+/-	+1	-	+2	+4	+3	+2	+2	+2	+3	

HOLE	10	11	12	13	14	15	16	17	18	**In**
PAR	4	3	4	3	4	4	4	4	5	35
NELSON	5	3	5	4	4	3	4	4	5	37
WOOD	5	4	5	3	5	3	4	3	5	37
+/-	+3	+4	+4	+3	+4	+4	+4	+3	+3	

NELSON	33–37	70
WOOD	36–37	73

Right: Byron's good friend "Jug" McSpaden, carrying the seat stick, marshalled for him in the playoff for the 1939 Open.

The Open Champ

$\mathcal{B}$yron Nelson, the mechanical golfer from Texas, had won his country's Open over a grueling 108 holes of play. With this one victory, Byron would prove to be one of the most popular U.S. Open Champions of all time.

Top photo: Byron and Louise on their way to the awards ceremony.

Left: Byron is congratulated by runner-up Craig Wood as Archie M. Reid, president of the United States Golf Association, looks on.

The 1940 PGA Championship

Hershey Country Club
Hershey, Pennsylvania
August 26 - September 2, 1940

The 1940 PGA Championship seemed to be played in a time warp as Walter Hagen, who first played in the PGA Championship in its inaugural year of 1916 and won in 1921, 1924, 1925, 1926 and 1927, advanced through the first two rounds of match play be-fore being edged by Jug Mc-Spaden 1 up in the third round.

Ben Hogan, in a portent of great things to come, easily moved through the first three rounds before being defeated by Ralph Guldahl in the quar-terfinal match.

Sam Snead defeated Nel-son Giddens 2 and 1 in the first round, Charles Sheppard 3 and 2 in the second round, Jimmy Hines 7 and 6 in the third round and Gene Sarazen—the winner of the 1922 and 1923 PGA Championships—1 up in the 36-hole quarterfinal match. In the semifinal match, Snead soundly beat Jug Mc-Spaden 5 and 4.

After qualifying for match play with a 151, Byron eased through the first round with a 4 and 3 win over Dick Shoemak-er, but in the second round, Byron barely survived a tough match against Frank Walsh and defeated him 1 up in 20 holes. In the third round, the first of the 36-hole matches, Byron defeated Dick Metz 2 and 1 in a close match. Then, he barely edged Ralph Guldahl 1 up on the 36th hole with the match all square after the 35th hole.

Top: Byron and Eddie Kirk cross their fingers for luck prior to their match in the fourth round of the PGA Championship at Hershey.

Middle: Byron met Ralph Guldahl in the semifinal match.

Right: Byron tees off on the fourth fairway in his tight semifinal match.

The Final Round

$\mathcal{T}$ he final round pitted the second place finishers in the last two PGA Championships—Byron Nelson, the runner-up to Henry Picard in a narrow 1-down loss in 1939, against long-hitting Sam Snead, the surprise loser against short-game maestro Paul Runyan in a whopping 8-and-7 loss in 1938.

Over the first 18 holes Byron took a 2-up lead by shooting a 71. Snead fought back in the afternoon shooting a fine 68.

The action intensified over the last three holes as Sam, with a 1-up lead on the 34th hole, barely missed a birdie from 20 feet, while Byron tapped in for his birdie from just two feet. All even now with just two holes to play, Sam hit his shot to six feet while Byron hit a magnificent wedge to within two feet. Snead narrowly missed his putt as Byron made his to go 1 up with just one hole to play.

On the final hole, uniquely a par-three, Byron hit his 3-iron to 10 feet. Sam missed his tee shot, ending off the green and proceed to mis-hit his second. Byron then two putted for his first PGA Championship.

It was a real donnybrook, with Byron just edging out his smooth swinging rival from West Virginia.

Byron pitches to the green.

Left: Byron drives from the 12th tee in the final match. Byron won 1 up over 36 holes.

At Last!

It was a sweet, but toughly contested, victory for Byron. After a narrow defeat in the 1939 PGA 1 up on the 37th hole by Henry Picard, Byron had captured the one championship that would prove to be problematical for him over the rest of his career.

1940 PGA

In Match Play Byron Defeated:

Dick Shoemaker, 4 and 3	First Round
Frank Walsh, 1 up (20 holes)	Second Round
Dick Metz, 2 and 1	Third Round
Eddie Kirk, 6 and 5	Quarterfinals
Ralph Guldahl, 1 up	Semifinals
Sam Snead, 1 up	Final

Top: Byron with runner-up "Slamming" Sammy Snead. PGA President Tom Walsh looks on.

Left: Following a disappointing loss the year before, Byron finally won the PGA Championship in 1940.

The 1942 Masters

Augusta National Golf Club
Augusta, Georgia
April 9–12, 1942

This was to be the last playing of The Masters until the end of World War II. And it proved to be one of the most memorable.

In the first round Horton Smith and Paul Runyan set the pace with five-under-par 67's and host Bobby Jones—coming out of retirement for his annual appearance, shot a par equaling 72, giving hope to the southern partisans who still vividly recalled the Grand Slam of just a dozen years earlier. Byron Nelson and ex-Yankee outfielder Sam Byrd were only one shot back of the leaders at four under.

Paired with Jimmy Thomson for the second round, Byron shot a superlative 67 to take a one-stroke lead going into the weekend. In the third round Byron posted an even-par 72 by putting well on the windswept devilishly fast greens, as Ben Hogan—the pre-tournament favorite—miraculously used only 28 putts to post a score of 67, just 3 behind Nelson. Bill Stern of NBC radio provided the nationwide broadcast for the very first time.

The *Augusta Chronicle* reported that the final round was a story of "…Hogan luck and Nelson misfortune, packed into a weird last nine, which brought them home all even after 72 holes…" All even with Byron playing the par-four ninth and Hogan playing two holes ahead, Byron canned a 25-footer on the ninth to re-gain a slim one-shot lead after struggling to simply make a bogey on the uphill par-five eighth.

Byron's lead ebbed and flowed as the players made their way through Amen Corner. On the 415-yard 11th hole Byron picked up another stroke taking a birdie 3 to Hogan's par. On the dogleg 13th Ben two putted for a bird, while Byron later made par. Hogan was over the back of the 15th, but his chip shot to the green caught the slick putting surface and ended up 20 feet away. Hogan made par as Nelson birdied some 20 minutes later. Now two strokes back and playing the 18th, Hogan hit his second to the green just six feet from the stick and made birdie, totaling a two-under 70 for the fourth round.

Needing two pars to win, Byron bogeyed the 17th from the front bunker. Now needing a birdie at the last to win and a par to force a playoff, Byron pushed his tee shot into the right trees into what one journalist called "heavy rough." Somehow he put his ball on the green 15 feet from the pin. As the first putt barely missed, he tapped in the second for a par.

An 18-hole playoff was scheduled for 2:30 on Monday afternoon.

Right: Jimmy Demaret, Byron Nelson and Ben Hogan meet
with tournament host Bobby Jones prior to the start of the 1942 Masters.

FRANK CHRISTIAN STUDIOS

The Playoff

*P*laying before a gallery of 4,000, Byron Nelson—after being up most of the previous night with a stomach ailment, began the playoff round with a double-bogey six as Ben Hogan carded a 4 after a picture-perfect drive of some 280 yards at the first hole.

Byron then proceeded to pick up six strokes to par over the next 12 holes. Beginning on the 525-yard par-five second hole, he placed his second shot 12 feet from the pin and two putted for a birdie 4.

On the uphill par-five eighth, Nelson outdrove Hogan, put his second a scant six feet away and holed it for eagle! With an eagle and three birdies in six holes, Byron now led by one.

1942 MASTERS	
*1. Byron Nelson	68 – 67 – 72 – 73 – 280
*1. Ben Hogan	73 – 70 – 67 – 70 – 280
3. Paul Runyan	67 – 73 – 72 – 71 – 283
4. Sam Byrd	68 – 68 – 75 – 74 – 285
5. Horton Smith	67 – 73 – 74 – 73 – 287
* Playoff	

Above: A nervous Byron with Ben Hogan just before the playoff began.

Left: Hogan tees off at the first hole of the playoff as Byron looks on.

A Classic Battle

On the downhill 10th Byron picked up another shot as Hogan bogeyed from off the green. At Amen Corner, both birdied the difficult 11th. Byron birdied the short 12th after a rifle-shot 7-iron to two feet to stretch his lead to two. Both birdied the beautiful par-five 13th. Byron had a three-stroke lead with five holes to play.

On the 14th Hogan continued his relentless pursuit with a bird from 15 feet as Byron made par. Byron's lead was now just two strokes with four holes to play. On the 15th Hogan made birdie as Byron three putted for his par. The lead had shrunk to just one shot.

The 16th proved to be the pivotal hole. Hogan, hitting first, pushed his tee shot into the pot bunker to the right of the green. Byron, with one of the great pressure shots of all time, hit his tee ball on the par three to within 30 inches of the cup. Hogan came out short and two putted for his bogey as Byron's putt somehow lipped out and he made three. The lead was now at two with two to play.

With par fours at the 17th—Byron's lead still at two, all that remained was the 18th. Hogan's drive was wild to the right and his second ended up in the bunker fronting the green. Byron hit a huge drive through the angle of the fairway, into what was then rough. His second was in the same bunker as Hogan's. Both Byron and Ben came out cleanly to eight feet. Byron, putting first, eased his putt up close for a bogey. Hogan made his putt for a par.

Byron had won the playoff by a single shot, shooting a 69 to Hogan's 70.

Byron putts during the playoff as Hogan carefully watches.

Byron comes out
of the sand to the home
green.

Phoenix Open

Phoenix Country Club
Phoenix, Arizona
January 12-14, 1945

"The record-shattering performances of Lord Byron were compiled over a backbreaking number of tournaments, bunched one upon the other, week after week. The surest method for appreciating Nelson's wondrous consistency is to travel the same tormenting grind that he did, tournament for tournament, trail for trail, total for total."
—Herbert Warren Wind, *The Story of American Golf*

*A*fter finishing second by one shot to Sam Snead at Los Angeles, Byron won the following week's event with a two-stroke victory over Denny Shute in the tourney sponsored by the Thunderbirds at the Phoenix Country Club.

Byron's score was a 10-under 274 over the flat, tree-bordered course. Denny Shute, the reigning PGA Champion, shot a pair of 68s in the last day's double round as Sam Byrd, the former major league baseball outfielder for the New York Yankees, shot a last-round 68 for a total of 277 and sole possession of third place. Jug McSpaden, Byron's good friend, finished fifth with a 283 aggregate. Sam Snead, suffering from putting woes, finished in 13th place with a 73 in the afternoon round.

As was the rule for the majority of the tournaments played during World War II, tournament prizes were paid off in War Bonds. Byron received one for $1,333 out of a total purse of $6,666.

PHOENIX OPEN	
1. Byron Nelson	68 – 65 – 72 – 69 – 274
2. Denny Shute	70 – 65 – 68 – 68 – 276
3. Sam Byrd	70 – 70 – 69 – 68 – 277
4. Bob Hamilton	68 – 70 – 75 – 65 – 278
5. Harold "Jug" McSpaden	70 – 65 – 76 – 72 – 283

#1

Corpus Christi Open

Corpus Christi Golf Club
Corpus Christi, Texas
February 2-4, 1945

*W*ith second-place finishes at both the Tucson Open and the Texas Open—both by narrow, one-stroke margins, Byron won the inaugural Corpus Christi Open by four strokes over his pal McSpaden, unofficially tying the world record of 264 set by Craig Wood at Forrest Hills in 1940. However, Fred Corcoran, the director of the PGA's tournament bureau, said that the mark would not be "official" since the course played under 6,000 yards.

Byron's morning round had five birdies and an eagle against two birdies, as McSpaden blazed through the morning's back nine in 30 strokes. His card for the morning included seven birdies and no bogeys.

Nevertheless, Byron bested a field that included Craig Wood, Johnny Revolta, Jimmy Demaret, Claude Harmon, Mike Turnesa, Sam Byrd and Bob Hamilton for his second win of 1945.

CORPUS CHRISTI OPEN	
1. Byron Nelson	66 – 63 – 65 – 70 – 264
2. Harold "Jug" McSpaden	65 – 69 – 63 – 71 – 268
3. Sam Schneider	68 – 68 – 65 – 68 – 269
3. Ky Laffoon	66 – 69 – 66 – 68 – 269
5. Craig Wood	64 – 68 – 70 – 68 – 270

Left: Byron bested his pal Jug McSpaden by four strokes in winning the 1945 Corpus Christi Open.

#2

New Orleans Open

New Orleans Country Club
(City Park No. 1 Course)
New Orleans, Louisiana
February 9-13, 1945

ied with Jug McSpaden after the first four rounds of the New Orleans Open at City Park No. 1 golf course at 284, Byron shot an unofficial course record of 32-33-65 to easily win the 18-hole playoff by five strokes as McSpaden scored 36-34-70, two under par.

Nelson's score in the playoff tied the course record set by Henry Picard in 1941, but it was not recognized as official as the players were permitted to tee the ball up in the fairways due to the inclement weather conditions. Byron's tee-to-green play was magnificent, as he hit only one bunker, yet made par from four feet on the 13th. His putting was equally as sharp, with only one blemish on his scorecard—a bogey on the 16th, after a three putt from 30 feet.

In all, Nelson had eight birdies as his friend placed second for the second consecutive year after leading the field with just the final 18 holes to be played.

NEW ORLEANS OPEN

*1. Byron Nelson	70 – 70 – 73 – 71 – 284	
*2. Harold "Jug" McSpaden	68 – 69 – 71 – 76 – 284	
3. Claude Harmon	70 – 71 – 73 – 75 – 289	
4. Sam Snead	78 – 70 – 73 – 69 – 290	
5. Johnny Bulla	71 – 71 – 76 – 73 – 291	

* Playoff	Nelson	65
	McSpaden	70

Left: Byron putts as his friend Jug McSpaden looks on. Although they tied for the lead at 284, Byron bested McSpaden in the playoff.

#3

Miami Four-Ball

Miami Springs Country Club
Miami, Florida
March 8-11, 1945

After consecutive second-place finishes to Sam Snead, first at the Gulfport Open and again the next week at the Pensacola Open, Byron tied for sixth at the Jacksonville Open as Snead won his third tournament in a row and his fourth of the new year.

With Snead on a winning tear, Byron began one of his own—one that would prove to be the most unassailable winning streak in all of sports history.

Paired with his pal McSpaden in the best-ball format, the duo of Nelson and McSpaden buzzed through the field as they defeated Willie Klein and Otey Crisman, Ben Hogan and Ed Dudley, Henry Picard and Johnny Revolta and finally Denny Shute and Sam Byrd in the 36-hole final.

Leaving their club pro jobs, Byron and Jug struck out on the Tour full-time armed with their new golf business contracts: Byron, the "Umbrella Man," and Jug, the advance man for Palm Beach clothes. Not only was Byron's fourth win of 1945 a portent of big things to come, but the concept of playing the tour on a full-time basis with business sponsors was to revolutionize the golf tour.

MIAMI FOUR-BALL

Nelson and McSpaden Defeated:

Klein and Crisman, 6 and 5	First Round
Hogan and Dudley, 4 and 3	Second Round
Picard and Revolta, 3 and 2	Semifinals
Shute and Byrd, 8 and 6	Final

Above: "The Gold Dust Twins" swept the field.

Left: Sam Byrd and Denny Shute met Jug McSpaden and Byron Nelson in the final.

#4

Charlotte Open

Myers Park Golf Club
Charlotte, North Carolina
March 16-21, 1945

*T*ied after the regulation four rounds with Sam Snead at 272, 16 under par, Byron and Sam again tied at 69 strokes each in the first playoff.

In the second playoff, Byron once again shaved another three strokes from par with a second consecutive 69 as Sam ran into putting woes once again and scored a one-over 73.

In referring to Byron, *The Charlotte Observer* wrote "His scintillating play added another amen to his reputation as golf's steadiest performer."

High praise indeed. But there was more, much more to come.

CHARLOTTE OPEN	
*1. Byron Nelson	70 – 68 – 66 – 68 – 272
*2. Sam Snead	65 – 68 – 69 – 70 – 272
3. Gene Kunes	68 – 72 – 70 – 69 – 279
4. Sam Byrd	67 – 72 – 70 – 71 – 280
5. Harold "Jug" McSpaden	66 – 70 – 68 – 77 – 281

* Playoff   First playoff: Second playoff:
                   Nelson 69   Nelson 69
                   Snead   69   Snead   73

Left: Byron outlasted Sam Snead in a playoff encompassing 36 holes at Charlotte.

#5

Greensboro Open

Starmount Country Club
Greensboro, North Carolina
March 23-25, 1945

The next week the tour moved on to Greensboro and the Starmount Country Club.

Byron's sterling play continued as he bested second-place finisher Sam Byrd by a whopping eight shots with a 68-66 final-day total to not only tie the course record, but record the lowest round of the tournament. With over 10,000 GI and civilian spectators out to watch, it was the largest crowd of the PGA winter circuit.

Sam Snead was 16 strokes back in sixth place, while four-ball partner Jug McSpaden was 23 strokes behind Byron in just 11th place! It almost seemed as if Byron was playing an easier golf course than the rest of his competitors.

The eight-stroke margin of victory was a record margin for the winter tour. It was Byron's sixth victory of the year.

GREENSBORO OPEN	
1. Byron Nelson	70 – 67 – 68 – 66 – 271
2. Sam Byrd	70 – 72 – 68 – 69 – 279
3. Johnny Revolta	68 – 70 – 71 – 71 – 280
4. Jimmy Hines	74 – 72 – 66 – 73 – 285
5. Craig Wood	72 – 68 – 73 – 73 – 286

Above: For the sixth time in 1945, Byron receives the winner's check. Unbelievably, this would be repeated 12 more times!

Left: Byron drives off the tee en route to his victory.

#6

Durham Open

Hope Valley Country Club
Durham, North Carolina
March 30 - April 1, 1945

yron swept what was referred to as the Tar Heel circuit in winning the Durham Open at Hope Valley Country Club over Toney Penna by five strokes, the third trick of the North Carolina swing of the tour. With a five-under 65 in his last round, he bested the course record of 67 set by Johnny Revolta the previous year and tied by amateur Ed Furgol earlier in the 1945 tournament.

Byron's wonderfully consistent play continued as he only missed two greens with his approach shots, in recording his course-record, final-round 65 on five birdies and thirteen pars.

Sam Snead's sporadic putting continued as he four putted the first hole in the final round and fell out of the running.

DURHAM OPEN	
1. Byron Nelson	71 – 69 – 71 – 65 – 276
2. Toney Penna	68 – 71 – 72 – 70 – 281
3. Jim Gauntt	72 – 70 – 70 – 70 – 282
4. Sam Byrd	70 – 71 – 69 – 75 – 285
5. Leonard Dodson	69 – 70 – 75 – 72 – 286

Byron won the Durham Open by five shots over Toney Penna to capture his third tournament in the state of North Carolina.

#7

Atlanta Open

Buckhead Lions Club
(Capital City Course)
Atlanta, Georgia
April 5-8, 1945

A s the Allies raced towards Berlin and the conclusion of the war, the 1945 Atlanta Open was played at the Capital City Course for a total purse of $10,000 worth of War Bonds.

Byron posted a 65 in the last round to win $2,000 in War Bonds by nine strokes with a 263 over Sam Byrd in second place at 272. Jug McSpaden finished in fifth place "just" 17 strokes back, as Sam Snead finished in sixth place, 18 back; Jimmy Demaret in 10th, 22 back and Ed "Porky" Oliver in 19th place, 31 strokes back. Future pros playing as amateurs included Ed Furgol at 287, and Fred Haas, Jr. at 289, good for 14th and 15th places respectively in the pro division.

By any estimation, Nelson's performance was almost unbelievable.

ATLANTA OPEN	
1. Byron Nelson	64 – 69 – 65 – 65 – 263
2. Sam Byrd	74 – 65 – 66 – 67 – 272
3. Jimmy Hines	73 – 69 – 71 – 65 – 278
4. Joe Kirkwood	72 – 69 – 68 – 70 – 279
5. Harold "Jug" McSpaden	69 – 75 – 68 – 68 – 280

Above: The winner by nine strokes.

Left: Byron receives the first-place prize of a $2,400 War Bond from tournament chairman R.J. Bicknell as PGA President Ed Dudley and fourth-round playing partner Jimmy Demaret look on.

#8

The "World Championship"

Fresh Meadow Country Club
Flushing, New York

Essex County Country Club
West Orange, New Jersey

May 26-27, 1945

*A*fter the Atlanta Open, there was a two-month break in the tour schedule. One of the exhibitions in which Nelson played during that time was a two-day challenge—pitting the two best players on the tour, Byron and Sam Snead—for what was billed as The "World Championship." On May 26, they played 36 holes at Fresh Meadow

Country Club in Flushing, New York, at stroke play; the next day, another 36 at Essex County Country Club, West Orange, New Jersey, at match play.

At Fresh Meadow, Snead led by three strokes after 18 holes. By the 14th hole, Nelson had gained three strokes, but a bogey at 17 again put him two back. At 18, Snead bogeyed, leaving Nelson with a long birdie putt for the tie. It missed by an inch. Snead won 143-144.

At Essex County, Nelson was 6 up after 13 holes. Then he three putted 16 and 18 to give two back. After lunch, they exchanged four holes before Snead birdied nine to get one back. But his bogey at 11 put Nelson 4 up again and he won at the 15th hole, 4 and 3.

Each had won one match. But, since Nelson's medal score for the first 36 holes plus the holes of the match itself was 272 vs. 276 for Snead, many pundits felt Nelson had effectively "won."

THE "WORLD CHAMPIONSHIP"		
	Stroke Play	Match Play
Byron Nelson	73 – 71 – 144	Won 4 and 3
Sam Snead	70 – 73 – 143	

Above: Byron comes out of the sand at Fresh Meadow.

Left: Nelson tees off as Snead watches.

Montreal Open

Islesmere Golf and Country Club
Montreal, Canada
June 7-10, 1945

*W*ith a four-under-par 68 in the final round of the Canadian PGA $10,000 tournament Byron Nelson shot a 268 total—20 under par—and set a new tournament record for play in Canada. Once again, Jug McSpaden placed second although 10 strokes back.

In Saturday's third round, McSpaden played brilliantly on the front, scoring 32. He had five birdies and one unbelievable bogey that included a shot from the rough ricocheting off a tree out of bounds and a 30-foot putt! On the back, Jug blew up, scoring a 41, for an unusual 73.

With typical modesty, Byron attributed his first round 63 to luck. But even though winter rules and preferred lies were in effect for the entire event, the course was certainly a tough one and definitely of championship caliber. 25,000 spectators were in attendance, an amazing number for that time.

MONTREAL OPEN		
1. Byron Nelson	63 – 68 – 69 – 68 – 268	
2. Harold "Jug" McSpaden	69 – 69 – 73 – 67 – 278	
3. Joe Zarhardt	70 – 73 – 69 – 71 – 283	
4. Ed Furgol*	70 – 69 – 71 – 74 – 284	
5. Jimmy Hines	69 – 74 – 72 – 72 – 287	
* Amateur		

Left: Byron comes out of the sand en route to victory number nine.

#9

Philadelphia Inquirer Invitational

Llanerch Country Club
Philadelphia, Pennsylvania
June 14-17, 1945

"…the most sensational finish of a career featuring dazzling comebacks"
The Philadelphia Inquirer, June 18, 1945

Harold "Jug" McSpaden, former head professional at the Philadelphia Country Club and still resident in the area, thought he had the tournament won as he started the back nine of the final round with a two-stroke lead at the Llanerch Country Club.

In a stunning finale, Byron recorded a 30 on the back nine for a new course record of 63, breaking the old mark of 66. His 269 aggregate was two strokes better than McSpaden's.

In analyzing his record-setting performance Byron remarked, "…it wasn't my driving, or my irons or my putting. It was my sand wedge. I played four short approaches with it that nearly holed out, on the 4th, 13th, 15th and 18th. The total of the four shots would hardly be six inches from the cups. One more turn and any of them would have dropped."

PHILADELPHIA INVITATIONAL	
1. Byron Nelson	68 – 68 – 70 – 63 – 269
2. Harold "Jug" McSpaden	73 – 66 – 66 – 66 – 271
3. Johnny Bulla	68 – 67 – 70 – 71 – 276
4. Bruce Coltart	70 – 68 – 73 – 68 – 279
5. Ed Furgol*	69 – 73 – 69 – 71 – 282
* Amateur	

Top: Always obliging, Byron signs an autograph for a young fan.

Above: Byron with "Jug" McSpaden and Ralph Guldahl.

Left: Byron comes out of the sand at Llanerch.

#10

PGA Championship

Moraine Country Club
Dayton, Ohio
July 9-15, 1945

*J*n the 36-hole qualifier Byron and sand play wizard Johnny Revolta tied for low at 138. With the cut at 147, missing the match play portion of the tournament were such notable players as former U.S. Open Champions Tony Manero and Craig Wood, as well as Jimmy Thomson and Joe Turnesa.

In the first round Byron, suffering from a pulled back muscle, defeated three-time PGA Champion Gene Sarazen 4 and 3 after falling behind early in the match. Jack Grout, later to gain fame as Jack Nicklaus' teacher, defeated the defending PGA Champion Bob Hamilton 5 and 4 while Byron's pal Jug McSpaden lost in an upset to little-known Clarence Doser 5 and 4.

Above: The famed Nelson finish with a driver at the 1945 PGA.

Left: The 1945 PGA Championship was the first tournament ever to use walkie-talkies as a means of communication.

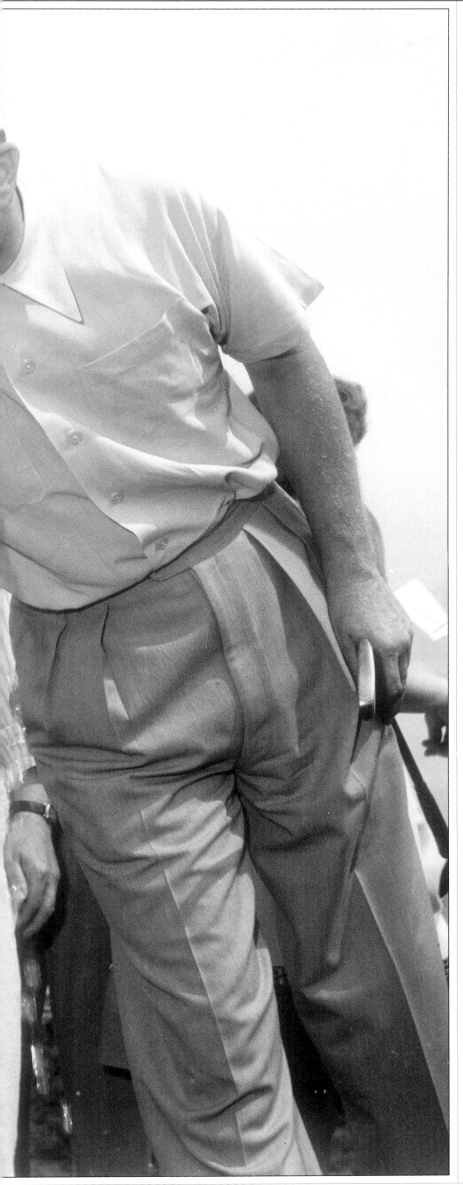

PGA Championship

*I*n the second round Byron just squeezed by Mike Turnesa 1 up after being 2 down with just four holes left to play. In the upset of the day, former Yankee outfielder Sam Byrd defeated former PGA Champ Johnny Revolta.

In the quarterfinals, Byron defeated two-time PGA Champion Denny Shute 3 and 2. For the sixth time in a row Byron had made the quarterfinals of the PGA Championship.

In the semifinals, Byron easily defeated Claude Harmon 5 and 4, while Sam Byrd beat Clarence Doser 7 and 6 in the upper bracket.

Top: Byron is congratulated by Denny Shute after defeating him 3 and 2 in the quarterfinals.

Above: Navigating out of the rough at Moraine.

Left: Byron takes a break during his quarterfinal match.

PGA Championship

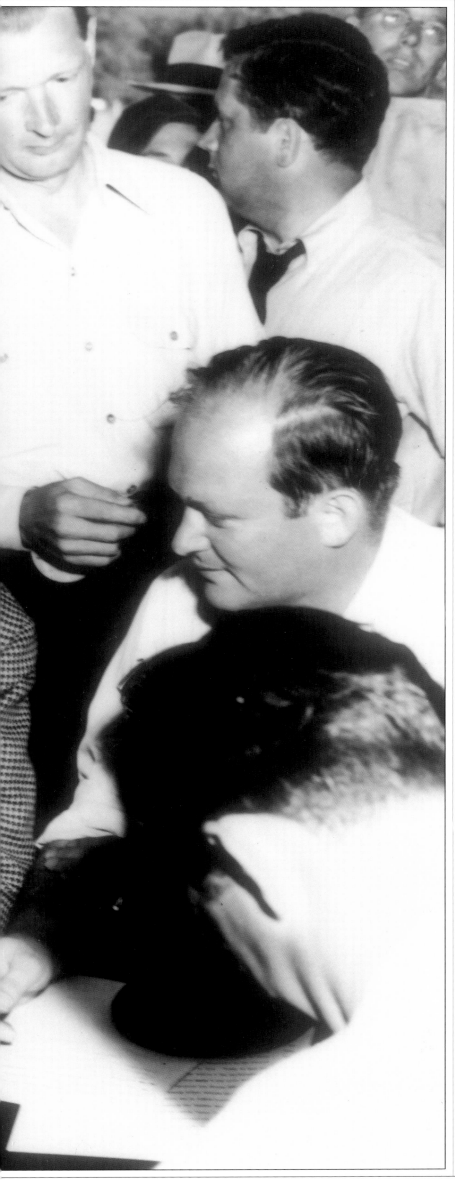

The final round matched Byron, in his fifth appearance in the finals, against former major league baseball star Sam Byrd. Byrd finished strongly in the morning 18 with four straight birdies to take a two-up lead into lunch. With an opening flurry, Byrd went par-par-birdie to gain another stroke after just three holes. Forever the competitor, Byron hung in and won the 22nd, 25th and 26th holes to even the match. He birdied the 29th and then proceeded to win the next three holes to wrap up the match, winning his second PGA Championship 4 and 3.

Byron was two under par for the day and a total of an almost unbelievable 37 under par for the 204 holes he played in the 1945 PGA.

Byron won his second PGA Championship in convincing fashion, the one tournament he considered his "jinx." With this win in the only major contested in 1945, the "streak" continued.

PGA CHAMPIONSHIP

In Match Play Byron Defeated:

Gene Sarazen, 4 and 3	First Round
Mike Turnesa, 1 up	Second Round
Denny Shute, 3 and 2	Quarterfinals
Claude Harmon, 5 and 4	Semifinals
Sam Byrd, 4 and 3	Final

Above: Byron with runner-up Sam Byrd and PGA President Ed Dudley.

Left: Byron is interviewed after his second PGA Championship victory.

#12

Tam O'Shanter Open

Tam O'Shanter Country Club
Chicago, Illinois
July 26–30, 1945

▶──◆──◀

*C*harlie Bartlett, the legendary golf writer for the *Chicago Daily Tribune*, best summarized Byron Nelson's amazing performance in the 1945 All-American Open:

"Surprise! John Byron Nelson, the man who even the gaffers of the Vardon-Hagen-Jones era now admit is the greatest golfer who ever swung a golf club, yesterday won his fourth and richest All-American Open golf championship in five years with a 72-hole score of 269 at the Tam O'Shanter Country Club. We thought you might be interested in the score first, the result being somewhat of a foregone conclusion."

"That 269, by the way, was 19 under par, and 11 ahead of the field of gents who nowadays feel they are playing for second money when they tee off against this Texas-born master of every stick in the game."

TAM O'SHANTER OPEN	
1. Byron Nelson	66 – 68 – 68 – 67 – 269
2. Lt. Ben Hogan	67 – 72 – 70 – 71 – 280
2. Gene Sarazen	70 – 68 – 72 – 70 – 280
4. Harold "Jug" McSpaden	71 – 69 – 68 – 73 – 281
4. Denny Shute	70 – 72 – 71 – 68 – 281
4. Vic Ghezzi	71 – 69 – 71 – 70 – 281

Top: Leading contenders and boyhood friends Ben Hogan and Byron Nelson discuss the tournament in the locker room.

Left: Byron receives the winner's check from Tournament founder George S. May.

#13

Canadian Open

Thornhill Golf Club
Toronto, Canada
August 2-4, 1945

*W*ith thirteen victories already in 1945 and the continuous win streak at 10, Byron had already lost some 12 pounds and his back was ailing. The Canadian Open, played at the tricky Thornhill course, was lengthened for the event and the par cut to 70.

Beginning with 68 in the first round and again in the last round, bracketed around a pair of 72s, Byron won the Canadian with an even-par total of 280, four strokes ahead of Herman Barron. Ed Furgol, who had a distinguished career as an amateur playing in the pro ranks and who turned pro himself several weeks earlier, finished third with a 285. Fred Haas , Jr. took top amateur honors at 289.

CANADIAN OPEN

1. Byron Nelson	68 – 72 – 72 – 68 – 280
2. Herman Barron	72 – 72 – 73 – 67 – 284
3. Ed Furgol	71 – 72 – 69 – 73 – 285
4. Vic Ghezzi	68 – 77 – 73 – 69 – 287
4. Jimmy Hines	72 – 76 – 72 – 67 – 287

Above: The crowds came out to watch Byron win his 14th tournament of 1945.

Left: The enthusiastic Canadians surrounded Byron after the victory.

#14

Esmeralda Open

Indian Canyon Course
Spokane, Washington
September 20-23, 1945

❦

The now repetitious pattern of Byron winning golf tournaments by a big margin over his rivals repeated itself once again at the Esmeralda Open in Spokane.

Great scoring was rampant on the final day as Byron set an unofficial PGA tournament record of 22 under par 266 with a 64 in the last round. (Because of playing preferred lies due to the sodden conditions, the record was deemed unofficial.)

Rival Sam Snead posted a new course record of 63 on the final day, the lowest round of the tournament, tying Ben Hogan for third spot at 275 as Jug McSpaden finished in second spot for the eighth time in 1945.

ESMERALDA OPEN	
1. Byron Nelson	66 – 66 – 70 – 64 – 266
2. Harold "Jug" McSpaden	70 – 68 – 69 – 66 – 273
3. Ben Hogan	70 – 66 – 68 – 71 – 275
3. Sam Snead	73 – 73 – 66 – 63 – 275
5. Ed Furgol	68 – 73 – 70 – 68 – 278
5. Jimmy Hines	72 – 69 – 72 – 65 – 278

Above: Byron signs autographs for servicemen on furlough.

Left: In a publicity shot, Byron astride the tournament mascot "Esmeralda."

#16

Seattle Open

Broadmoor Golf Club
Seattle, Washington
October 11-14, 1945

hree weeks earlier at the Portland Invitational, Ben Hogan established a new PGA four-round mark of 261 shooting rounds of 65-69-63-64 as Byron—13 strokes under par for the tournament—placed second an incredible 14 shots behind Hogan.

With rounds of 62-68-63-66-259 at Seattle, Byron broke Hogan's record in convincing fashion.

Alex Rose, writing in the *Seattle Post-Intelligencer* best summarized Byron's record-shattering performance: "Nelson's golf yesterday was much like what he had on tap throughout the entire tournament—almost flawless. He was down the middle with his wood and iron tee shots and from there on his play was just as uncannily accurate. Sure, he slipped a wee bit here and there—but he gave galleryites the greatest exhibition of shotmaking the world has ever seen from the time he hit his first shot from No. 1 last Thursday morning until he holed out on the 18th last evening to establish his record."

SEATTLE OPEN	
1. Byron Nelson	62 – 68 – 63 – 66 – 259
2. Harry Givan*	66 – 65 – 71 – 70 – 272
2. Harold "Jug" McSpaden	70 – 71 – 64 – 67 – 272
4. Ed Furgol	68 – 69 – 67 – 71 – 275
4. Jimmy Hines	69 – 69 – 66 – 71 – 275
* Amateur	

Above: Byron with runner-up amateur Harry Givan.

Left: Byron posts a new PGA record.

#17

Glen Garden Invitational

Glen Garden Country Club
Fort Worth, Texas
December 14-16, 1945

*A*s a fitting climax to the record-smashing year, Byron returned to Fort Worth and the Glen Garden Country Club where he and Ben Hogan were first introduced to the game as caddies.

Overcoming cold weather, Byron finished eight strokes ahead of fellow Texan Jimmy Demaret at 281 and nine strokes in front of Jug McSpaden in third place. Sam Snead ended up in fifth as Ben Hogan finished seventh.

One can only wonder, had Hogan and Nelson tied after the regulation four rounds, what the playoff would have been like. Would they have swapped their prizes as they had done when they played for the Glen Garden Caddie Championship?

GLEN GARDEN INVITATIONAL	
1. Byron Nelson	72 – 65 – 66 – 70 – 273
2. Jimmy Demaret	71 – 67 – 74 – 69 – 281
3. Harold "Jug" McSpaden	73 – 70 – 74 – 65 – 282
4. "Dutch" Harrison	69 – 70 – 73 – 71 – 283
5. Sam Snead	73 – 68 – 74 – 71 – 286
5. Johnny Bulla	73 – 72 – 73 – 68 – 286

Above: Boyhood friends and fellow caddies return to Glen Garden.

Left: Walter Hagen presents the winner's check to Byron and the runner-up check to Jimmy Demaret.

#18

Swing Analysis

By Ken Venturi

Ken Venturi

*B*yron has been mentor and teacher to many young players. However, his most famous pupils have been Frank Stranahan, Harvie Ward, Ken Venturi and Tom Watson.

Nelson gave lessons to Stranahan soon after he became the pro at Inverness in 1940. Stranahan later won two British Amateur titles and many important U.S. amateur events.

Ken Venturi and Byron first met at the 1952 U.S. Amateur in Portland, Oregon. Afterwards, Byron asked if Ken would like to work with him on his game. Ken enthusiastically agreed and a game was set up at the San Francisco Golf Club shortly thereafter. Ken shot a superlative round of 66 and was expecting Byron to heap praise on him. Rather, Byron said that they had seven or eight things to work on and would get started the next morning. Such was the beginning of a wonderful relationship that endures to this day.

Despite physical problems that foreshortened his career, Ken won the 1964 U.S. Open at Congressional in one of the most heroic final rounds in the annals of golf history.

Not long after he started with Venturi, Nelson helped Ward, who at that time couldn't work the ball left or right. Nelson taught him how, and Ward went on to win both the American and British Amateurs.

(Top) Ken Venturi and Byron Nelson in the 1950s.

(Left) Byron monitors Ken Venturi's swing on the practice tee.

One Incredible Four-Ball!

S oon after the San Francisco Amateur, in which Ken Venturi had beaten Harvie Ward in the final, Eddie Lowery, Byron Nelson and their wives—in Pebble Beach for the 1956 Crosby "Clambake"—were invited to dinner at George Coleman's house. (Lowery, a San Francisco auto dealer and a good friend of Byron's, first gained golfing fame as Francis Ouimet's young, diminutive caddy in his 1913 U.S. Open victory.)

Coleman remarked over cocktails to Lowery, "Those kids played really well in San Francisco." Since Venturi and Ward had gone to work for Lowery at his dealership, he replied proudly, "They can beat anybody in the world."

"Anybody?" asked Coleman. "Yes, anybody," replied Lowery.

"How about Hogan and Nelson?" challenged Coleman. The match was set for 11 o'clock the next day at Cypress Point.

Hogan—not wanting to be seen playing against amateurs—was concerned that the match would draw a crowd. So he booked a diversionary starting time in all their names at Pebble Beach for the same time the match was actually to be played next door. The match proved to be one for the ages.

Incredibly, just three holes were halved in pars. The rest were halved or won with birdies or better.

After nine holes, the match was all even. On the 10th hole, Hogan chipped in from about 70 feet for an eagle. The next four holes were halved. Hogan, and then Venturi, birdied fifteen, and the pros remained 1 up. On the 16th and 17th, Ward and Nelson both birdied to leave the amateurs 1 down going to the final hole.

After good drives, Venturi placed his approach 12 feet from the flag. Hogan put it inside him to 10 feet. Venturi proceeded to hole his birdie putt. Nelson turned to Hogan and said, "Knock it in, Ben, and we win." Hogan replied, "I'm not about to be halved by two amateurs!" He then winked at Venturi before canning the putt for a birdie 3 and the match.

What a match! Neither team was ever more than one down as Hogan shot 63, Nelson 67, Venturi 65, and Ward 67. Between them, they had 27 birdies and one eagle.

In later years, the match achieved mythic proportions with reports of an incredible amount of money being wagered. To this day, Venturi claims it was only a small Nassau.

But who wouldn't have paid big money to have witnessed it!

Right: The dramatic beauty of Cypress Point was a fitting backdrop to the Hogan-Nelson/Venturi-Ward four-ball match. Pictured here is the 16th hole, which both Byron and Harvey Ward halved with birdies.

Tom Watson

⊢—▸—◦—◂—⊣

Byron first met Watson at Doral in 1973, and offered to work with him after Watson lost the U.S. Open at Winged Foot in the following year. They became fast friends.

At the 1975 British Open at Carnoustie, the weather on the day of the last round was windy, rainy and cold. Nelson told Watson how he had played the same course in 1937 under similar conditions, and added, "Even if you make three bogeys in a row, don't think anything about it, because everyone will be making bogies." Watson actually did, at one point, make three bogies in a row, but didn't let it bother him. He tied Jack Newton, and later won in a playoff.

However, it was not until 1976, after a winless year for Watson on tour, that the pair began working together regularly. Since then, Watson has won four more British Opens, two Masters, a U.S. Open and 28 other tour events.

And more importantly, they became great friends.

(Right) Byron Nelson scrutinizes Tom Watson's sand play.

Left: The 1947 U.S. Ryder Cup Team: (left to right, seated) Herman Barron, Jimmy Demaret, Ben Hogan, Ed Oliver, Lew Worsham; (standing) "Dutch" Harrison, Lloyd Mangrum, Herman Kaiser, Byron Nelson and Sam Snead.

Below: Members of the strong 1965 American Ryder Cup Team (from top of stairs): Johnny Pott, Ken Venturi, Julius Boros, Tommy Jacobs, Gene Littler, Billy Casper, Arnold Palmer, Don January and Dave Marr (partially hidden). Byron is greeted by Lord Derby, President of the British PGA. Team member Tony Lema was en route.

Ryder Cup
1937, 1947 – Team Member
1965 – Captain

Nelson first played Ryder Cup golf when he was a member of the victorious 1937 U.S. team. The PGA later picked him for the 1939 and 1941 teams, but these teams never got to play because of World War II.

Even though Byron had retired in 1946, the PGA once again selected him as a member of the 1947 team that played the British at Portland (Oregon) Golf Club. The U.S. won comfortably, 11½ points to 1. This is the only time a retired player was picked for the Ryder Cup!

In an amusing incident from these matches, Herman Barron and Nelson were 1 up against Dai Rees and Sam King in the foursomes going to 17, a par-three hole. Nelson put his tee shot eight feet from the hole; the British were 15 feet away. Byron, recognizing that Barron was a superb putter, conceded the Britishers' putt. Although Barron thought Nelson had lost his senses to concede such a long putt, he made the putt to close out the match 2 and 1.

The next day, in the singles, Nelson defeated Arthur Lees by the same margin.

In 1965, Nelson was non-playing captain of the U.S. team that met the British at Royal Birkdale. As usual, he gave sound advice exactly when needed. Just before the match, Lema came up to him, saying, "Byron, I'm driving badly—I need help." Nelson soon saw that Lema was not setting the club properly at the top of the swing. He explained this, and Lema immediately played better.

The U.S. won the match 19½ to 12½.

Masters Bridge Dedication

*I*t was certainly an honor of the highest caliber when Bob Jones and Cliff Roberts decided to dedicate the bridge, leading from the 13th tee across Rae's Creek to the fairway, in honor of Byron's spectacular play on the 12th and 13th holes in winning the 1937 Masters. On hand for the ceremony was Ben Hogan, for whom the bridge leading to the 12th green (in the foreground of the large picture at left) was also dedicated.

(Above) The plaque commemorating Byron's feats on the 12th and 13th holes in winning the 1937 Masters.

(Below) Bob Jones and Cliff Roberts with Byron Nelson and Ben Hogan shortly after the dedication ceremony.

(Left) Amen Corner (from left to right): the 11th green, the Hogan bridge, the 12th green, the 13th tee and the Nelson Bridge.

The Complete Record of Byron Nelson

>———‹♦›•‹○›•‹♦›———<

Researched and Compiled by Sal Johnson

1 9 3 2

1932 Texarkana*	3					296	$ 75.00
				1932 Earnings			**$75.00**

1 9 3 3

1933 Los Angeles Open	T14		147	76	71	294	$ 34.50
1933 Agua Caliente Open	T31		230	74		304	0.00
1933 Arizona Open	T8		147	73	71	291	NA
1933 Western Open	T7	74	73	74	74	295	NA
1933 Miami Biltmore Open	T29	74	79	76	76	305	50.00
				1933 Earnings			**$84.50**

1 9 3 4

1934 Los Angeles Open	T26					297	$ 36.00
1934 San Francisco Match Play	T17		Lost in second round				55.75
1934 Agua Caliente Open*	T23	75	73	70	76	294	33.33
1934 Texas Open	T2		136	74	74	284	325.00
1934 Galveston Open	2					293	325.00
1934 U.S. Open	CUT	79	83			162	0.00
1934 Pasadena Open	T22	73	72	70	78	293	0.00
1934 California Open	T4	75	70	73	69	287	NA
				1934 Earnings			**$775.08**

1 9 3 5

1935 Riverside Pro-Am*	T-2	64				64	$125.00
1935 Los Angeles Open	T40	74	75	80	74	303	0.00
1935 San Francisco Match Play	T5		Lost in quarterfinals				154.00
1935 Sacramento Open		75	72	80	80	307	NA
1935 Glen Dale Open						297	NA
1935 Agua Caliente Open	T6	72	71	76	72	291	257.00
1935 Phoenix Open	T10	72	73	71	74	290	75.00
1935 Tournament of the Gardens	6	73	71	70	70	284	100.00
1935 North and South Open	12	71	69	77	76	293	60.00
1935 Atlanta Open	3	71	75	69		215	250.00
1935 Masters	T9	71	74	72	74	291	137.50
1935 Metropolitan Open		76	76	77	77	306	NA
1935 Philadelphia PGA		75	75	73		223	NA
1935 U.S. Open	T32	75	81	82	77	315	0.00
1935 Sweckly Open		74	78			152	NA
1935 Western Open	3	75	72	74	75	296	200.00
1935 Medinah Open	T12	78	73	77	73	301	62.50
1935 General Brock Hotel Open	T2	72	71	72	77	292	600.00
1935 St. Paul Open		72	76	73	76	297	NA
1935 New Jersey State Open*	1	75	71	70	72	288	400.00
1935 True Temper Open		75	76	75	79	305	NA
1935 Hershey Open	T6	71	74	73	78	296	143.75
1935 Glens Falls Open	T12	74	72	71	73	290	56.00
1935 Calvert Open	T10	76	73	75	71	295	25.00
1935 PGA Championship (Match Play)		Shot 156, did not qualify for match play					
1935 Jersey PGA	2	71	74	71	75	291	100.00

1 9 3 5 (continued)

1935 Metropolitan Open	Cut	80	75			155	0.00
1935 Louisville Open	T4	71	74	72	72	289	362.50
1935 Orlando Open		72	75	73	77	297	NA
1935 Sarasota Open		73	69	68	77	287	NA
1935 Miami Biltmore Open	T29	70	72	77	75	294	37.00
1935 Pasadena Open	T18	71	75	73	71	290	50.00
				1935 Earnings			**$3,195.25**

1 9 3 6

1936 Riverside Open	T3	72	69	71	74	286	$300.00
1936 Los Angeles Open	7	68	72	72	75	287	200.00
1936 Sacramento Open	3	75	69	71	72	287	350.00
1936 San Francisco Match Play	Shot 147, did not qualify for match play						52.50
1936 Catalina Open	T6	65	65	64	65	259	208.34
1936 Thomasville Open	WD	75	75			150	
1936 St. Petersburg Open	T12	71	79	73	69	292	55.00
1936 Hollywood Open	T22	71	73	72	71	287	
1936 St. Augustine Pro-Am* (Match Play)		Won one match					50.00
1936 Tournament of the Gardens	T11	75	71	77	73	296	75.00
1936 North and South Open		79	75	76	76	306	
1936 Masters	T13	76	71	77	74	298	50.00
1936 Metropolitan Open	1	71	69	72	71	283	750.00
1936 U.S. Open	CUT	79	74			153	
1936 Shawnee Open	T4	72	71	73	74	290	226.00
1936 General Brock Open	10	74	72	76	74	296	140.00
1936 Illinois Open	7	75	69			144	21.66
1936 Western Open	3	69	72	72	65	278	200.00
1936 St. Paul Open	T5	68	72	71	70	281	306.00
1936 Vancouver Jubilee Open	T2	70	70	72	66	278	975.00
1936 Victoria Open	2	64	68	69	71	272	450.00
1936 Seattle Open	7	73	74	74	73	293	270.00
1936 Portland Open	T7	71	68	71	72	282	250.00
1936 Glens Falls Open	3	66	73	75	70	284	400.00
1936 Hershey Open	T9	73	74	73	73	293	180.00
1936 Canadian Open	T10	72	71	75	69	287	41.66
1936 New Jersey Pro Amateur							75.00
1936 New Jersey PGA	3					293	75.00
1936 PGA Championship (Match Play)		Shot 158, did not qualify for match play					0.00
1936 Augusta Open	T14	71	71	74	73	289	86.25
1936 Miami Biltmore Open	T43	75	76	72	77	300	0.00
				1936 Earnings			**$5,787.41**

1 9 3 7

1937 Los Angeles Open	T9	73	71	70	71	285	$ 75.00
1937 Oakland Open	T17	75	70	66	73	284	NA
1937 Sacramento Open	6	69	75	70	71	287	140.00
1937 San Francisco Match Play	T5		Lost in second round				150.00
1937 Houston Open	T4	70	73	74	68	285	250.00
1937 Thomasville Open	T14	76	73	70	73	292	32.00
1937 St. Petersburg Open	T14	71	69	74	77	291	15.00
1937 Florida West Coast Open	T2	73	70	72	74	289	400.00

Year	Tournament	Place	R1	R2	R3	R4	Total	Earnings
1937	Hollywood Open	T5	68	71	70	68	277	200.00
1937	Miami Int'l. Four-Ball* *(Match Play)* *(with Jug McSpaden)*	T9		Lost in first round				NA
1937	St Augustine Pro-Am*	T9						50.00
1937	North and South Open	3	68	71	78	75	292	500.00
1937	Masters	1	66	72	75	70	283	1,500.00
1937	PGA Championship *(Match Play)*	T5		Lost in quarterfinals				200.00
1937	U.S. Open	T20	73	78	71	73	295	50.00
1937	British Open	5	75	76	71	74	296	125.00
1937	Central Pennsylvania*	1	69	71			140	150.00
1937	Hershey						306	0.00
1937	Belmont Country Club *(Match Play)*	1						2,500.00
1937	Miami Biltmore Open	11	74	70	70	75	289	125.00
1937	Nassau Open	T13	70	75	70	70	285	47.50
1937	Argentine Open Championship*	T6					294	NA

1937 Earnings **$6,509.50**

1938

Year	Tournament	Place	R1	R2	R3	R4	Total	Earnings
1938	Los Angeles Open	T49	71	72	72	77	292	$ 0.00
1938	Del Mar Pro-Am		80	76			156	NA
1938	Pasadena Open	3	73	71	64	71	279	350.00
1938	Oakland Open		75	71	71	79	296	NA
1938	Sacramento Open	T8	75	75	74	70	294	100.00
1938	San Francisco Match Play	T16		Lost in first round				75.00
1938	New Orleans	Cut	79	77	77	73	306	0.00
1938	Thomasville Open	1	66	73	71	70	280	700.00
1938	St. Petersburg Open	3	72	71	69	71	283	350.00
1938	Hollywood Open	1	71	68	69	67	275	700.00
1938	Miami Int'l. Four-Ball* *(Match Play)* *(with Jug McSpaden)*	T3		Lost in semifinals				150.00
1938	North and South Open	T3	69	72	71	74	286	400.00
1938	Greensboro Open		80	71	75	70	296	NA
1938	Masters	5	73	74	70	73	290	400.00
1938	U.S. Open	T5	77	71	74	72	294	412.50
1938	PGA Championship *(Match Play)*	T5		Lost in quarterfinals				250.00
1938	Central Pennsylvania*	2	66	75			141	90.00
1938	Hershey Four-Ball *(with Ed Dudley)*	T3						325.00
1938	Westchester 108 Hole Open	T3	294		69	71	434	900.00
1938	Columbia Open	T6	75	73	72	73	293	NA
1938	Augusta Open	T8	73	72	70	73	288	NA
1938	Miami Open	Cut	77	76			153	0.00
1938	Houston Open	T5	77	75	67		219	186.66
1938	Cleveland Open	T20	69	74	75	73	291	100.00

1938 Earnings **$5,489.16**

1939

Year	Tournament	Place	R1	R2	R3	R4	Total	Earnings
1939	Los Angeles Open	T7	72	70	74	70	286	$ 129.25
1939	Oakland Open	9	72	69	70	69	280	230.00
1939	San Francisco Match Play	T17		Lost in first round				75.00
1939	Bing Crosby Pro-Am*	T2	68	71			139	300.00
1939	Texas Open	3	67	69	69	69	274	550.00
1939	Phoenix Open	1	68	65	65		198	700.00
1939	New Orleans Open	T5	74	73	69	75	291	650.00
1939	Thomasville Open	T4	72	74	69		215	183.34
1939	St. Petersburg Open	T4	70	71	70		211	250.00
1939	Miami-Biltmore Four-Ball *(Match Play)* *(with Frank Walsh)*	T9		Lost in first round				50.00
1939	Seminole Invitational*	1	68				68	565.00
1939	Indian Creek Open	1	73				73	25.00
1939	St Augustine Open*							75.00
1939	North and South Open	1	71	68	70	71	280	1,000.00
1939	Greensboro Open	10	73	73	70	74	290	170.00
1939	Masters	7	71	69	72	75	287	250.00
1939	U.S. Open	1	72	73	71	68	284	1,000.00
1939	Inverness Invitational Four-Ball* *(with Jug McSpaden)*	T2	+4					412.50
1939	Massachusetts Open	1	70	71	71	71	283	400.00
1939	Scranton Open	T19	146	71	74		291	35.00
1939	PGA Championship *(Match Play)*	2		Lost in final				600.00

Year	Tournament	Place	R1	R2	R3	R4	Total	Earnings
1939	Western Open	1	69	71	70	71	281	750.00
1939	St. Paul Open	T10	68	73	66	74	281	205.00
1939	Dapper Dan Open	T8	72	71	72	75	291	391.66
1939	Central Pennsylvania Open*	1	68	69			137	100.00
1939	Berkshire Pro-Am*	1	66	68	68	69	271	140.00
1939	Walter Hagen 25th Anniversary* *(with Dick Metz)*	3	+4					400.00
1939	Miami Four-Ball* *(Match Play)*	1						75.00
1939	Seminole Pro-Am*							20.00
1939	Indian Creek*							25.00
1939	Thomasville Open	2	68	68	69		205	450.00
1939	Hershey Open	4	68	73	71	75	287	450.00
1939	Philadelphia PGA	1	69	68			137	100.00
1939	Miami Open	5	68	69	68	73	278	600.00

1939 Earnings **$11,356.75**

1940

Year	Tournament	Place	R1	R2	R3	R4	Total	Earnings
1940	Los Angeles Open	WD	74				74	$ 0.00
1940	Oakland Open	WD						0.00
1940	San Francisco Match Play	T5		Lost in quarterfinals				150.00
1940	Crosby Open	WD	74				74	0.00
1940	Phoenix Open		74	73	68		215	NA
1940	Texas Open	1	68	67	69	67	271	1,120.00
1940	Houston Open	WD	78				78	0.00
1940	New Orleans Open	T15	74	73	78	70	295	146.00
1940	St. Petersburg Open	2	71	72	69		212	450.00
1940	Miami Four-Ball* *(Match Play)* *(with Jug McSpaden)*	T5		Lost in second round				100.00
1940	Thomasville Open	2	68	68	69		205	450.00
1940	North and South Open	3	70	72	74	70	286	500.00
1940	Greensboro Open	T3	73	74	68	68	280	412.50
1940	Asheville "Land of the Sky" Open	T7	67	74	71	72	284	230.00
1940	Masters	3	69	72	74	70	285	600.00
1940	Ohio Open*	1	72	69	72	71	284	250.00
1940	Goodall Palm Beach Round Robin	6	+2					375.00
1940	U.S. Open	T5	72	74	70	74	290	325.00
1940	Inverness Invitational Four-Ball	T7	−14					175.00
1940	PGA Championship *(Match Play)*	1						1,100.00
1940	Anthracite Open	2		142	70	66	278	750.00
1940	Miami Open	1	69	65	67	70	271	2,537.50

1940 Earnings **$9,671.00**

1941

Year	Tournament	Place	R1	R2	R3	R4	Total	Earnings
1941	Los Angeles Open		72	77	75	78	302	$ 0.00
1941	Oakland Open						290	0.00
1941	San Francisco Match Play		Shot 147, did not qualify for match play					0.00
1941	Bing Crosby Pro-Am	T5	68	71			139	125.00
1941	Phoenix Western Open	T2	68	69	67	74	278	600.00
1941	Texas Open	T4	71	71	69	71	282	325.00
1941	New Orleans Open	T8	75	69	69	72	285	210.00
1941	Thomasville Open	T6	73	70	74		217	170.00
1941	St. Petersburg Open	T13	74	70	65	77	286	40.00
1941	Miami Four-Ball *(Match Play)* *(with Jug McSpaden)*	T5		Lost in second round				75.00
1941	Seminole Pro-Am*	1	64	70			134	803.29
1941	Florida West Coast Open	2	72	67	67		206	500.00
1941	North and South Open	T4	69	71	69	76	285	350.00
1941	Winston-Salem Pro-Am*		65	71			136	133.33
1941	Greensboro Open	1	72	64	70	70	276	1,200.00
1941	Asheville Open	T10	74	76	74	72	296	155.00
1941	Masters	2	71	69	73	70	283	800.00
1941	U.S. Open	T17	73	73	74	77	297	50.00
1941	PGA Championship *(Match Play)*	2						600.00
1941	Inverness Four-Ball *(with Jimmy Thomson)*	2	+8					600.00
1941	St. Paul Open	T7	73	70	70	68	281	277.50
1941	Toledo District Open		71	68				75.00
1941	Mahoning Open	2	67	70	73	67	277	750.00
1941	Tam O'Shanter Open	1	67	69	72	70	278	2,000.00
1941	Henry Hurst Invitational	T6	71	72	74	68	285	350.00

Year	Tournament	Place	R1	R2	R3	R4	Total	Earnings
1941	Ohio Open*	1	68	69	72	62	271	125.00
1941	Miami Open	1	70	67	66	66	269	2,537.50
1941	Harlingen Open	4	65	70	70	66	271	450.00
1941	Beaumont Open	T7	71	69	74	72	286	225.00
1941	St. Augustine Pro-Amateur	17						NA

1941 Earnings $13,526.62

1942

Year	Tournament	Place	R1	R2	R3	R4	Total	Earnings
1942	Los Angeles Open	T6	72	74	70	72	288	$ 350.00
1942	Oakland Open	1	67	69	69	69	274	1,000.00
1942	San Francisco Open	8					287	200.00
1942	Bing Crosby Pro-Am	T14	70	72			142	57.00
1942	Western Open - Phoenix	T11	72	68	73	72	285	105.00
1942	Texas Open	T8	74	67	73	70	284	162.50
1942	New Orleans Open	6	74	73	69	71	287	300.00
1942	St. Petersburg Open	T2	68	76	75	70	289	585.33
1942	Miami Four-Ball (with Henry Picard)	5	Lost in second round					100.00
1942	Seminole Pro-Am*		74	72			146	50.00
1942	North and South Open	T3	69	70	69	73	281	500.00
1942	Greensboro Open	T4	72	68	68	74	282	412.50
1942	Asheville "Land of the Sky" Open	3	69	73	66	70	278	550.00
1942	Masters	1	68	67	72	73	280	1,500.00
1942	PGA Championship (Match Play)	T3	Lost in semifinals					700.00
1942	Inverness Four-Ball (with Jimmy Thomson)	T4	+5					450.00
1942	Hale America Open	T4	69	70	69	70	278	475.00
1942	Tam O'Shanter Open	1	67	71	65	77	280	2,500.00
1942	Toledo Open*	1						NA
1942	Ohio Open*	1					273	NA

1942 Earnings $9,997.33

1943

Year	Tournament	Place	R1	R2	R3	R4	Total	Earnings
1943	All-American Open	T3	72	72	71	68	283	$900.00
1943	Chicago Victory Open	5	68	72	72	72	284	0.00
1943	Minneapolis Four-Ball (with Jug McSpaden)	2	+8					NA
1943	Kentucky Open	1						NA
1943	Golden Valley Invitational*	2						NA

1943 Earnings $900.00

1944

Year	Tournament	Place	R1	R2	R3	R4	Total	Earnings
1944	Los Angeles Open	T3	68	72	71	72	283	$1,125.00
1944	San Francisco Victory Open	1	68	69	68	70	275	2,400.00
1944	Phoenix Open	2	71	66	71	65	273	750.00
1944	Texas Open	T2	75	63	68	68	274	650.00
1944	New Orleans Open	2	71	78	71	70	290	750.00
1944	Gulfport Open – Mississippi	3	73	70	69	71	283	550.00
1944	Charlotte Open	3	70	70	73	66	279	1,000.00
1944	Durham Open	2	68	67	69	70	274	750.00
1944	Knoxville War Bond Tournament	1	69	68	66	67	270	1,333.00
1944	Philadelphia Inquirer	6	70	71	69	79	289	675.00
1944	New York*	1						500.00
1944	New York Red Cross Tourney	1	69	69	66	71	275	2,666.65
1944	Chicago Victory Open	3	65	74	68	69	276	1,350.00
1944	Minneapolis Four-Ball* (with Jug McSpaden)	1	+13					800.00
1944	Utah Open*	2	67	65	72	69	273	450.00
1944	Beverly Hills	1	71	69	68	69	277	1,500.00
1944	PGA Championship (Match Play)	2	Lost in final					1,500.00
1944	Tam O'Shanter Open	1	68	70	73	69	280	10,100.00
1944	Nashville Open	1	64	67	68	70	269	2,400.00
1944	Texas Victory Open	1	69	69	70	68	276	2,000.00
1944	Portland Open	T4	73	74	75	74	296	1,025.00
1944	San Francisco Open (Match Play)	1	72	71	69	69	281	2,666.70
1944	Oakland Open	T6	66	72	72	73	283	380.00
1944	Richmond Open	T3	73	69	68	70	280	667.67

1944 Earnings $37,982.02

1945

Year	Tournament	Place	R1	R2	R3	R4	Total	Earnings
1945	Los Angeles Open	T2	71	72	70	71	284	$1,600.00
1945	Phoenix Open	1	68	65	72	69	274	1,333.00
1945	Tucson Open	2	67	68	67	67	269	700.00
1945	Texas Open	2	67	66	68	68	269	700.00
1945	Corpus Christi Open	1	66	63	65	70	264	1,000.00
1945	New Orleans Open	1	70	70	73	71	349	1,333.33
1945	Gulfport Open	2	69	68	72	66	346	700.00
1945	Pensacola Open Invitational	2	69	69	71	65	274	700.00
1945	Jacksonville Open	T6	68	66	72	69	275	380.00
1945	Miami Int'l. Four-Ball* (Match Play)	1	21 up in four matches					1,500.00
1945	Charlotte Open	1	70	66	68	68	272	2,000.00
1945	Greensboro Open	1	70	67	68	66	271	1,333.00
1945	Durham Open	1	71	69	71	65	276	1,333.00
1945	Atlanta Open	1	64	69	65	65	263	2,000.00
1945	Montreal Open	1	63	68	69	68	268	2,000.00
1945	Philadelphia Inquirer	1	68	68	70	63	269	3,333.33
1945	Chicago Victory National Open	1	69	68	68	70	275	2,000.00
1945	PGA Championship (Match Play)	1						5,000.00
1945	Tam O'Shanter Open	1	66	68	68	67	269	13,600.00
1945	Canadian Open	1	68	72	72	68	280	2,000.00
1945	Spring Lake Pro-Member*	1	140		140			2,100.00
1945	Memphis Invitational	T4	69	73	66	68	276	1,200.00
1945	Knoxville Invitational	1	67	69	73	67	276	2,666.67
1945	Nashville Invitational	T2	70	64	67	68	269	1,600.00
1945	Dallas Open	3	72	70	71	68	281	1,333.33
1945	Tulsa Open	4	73	69	75	71	288	800.00
1945	Esmeralda Open	1	66	66	70	64	266	2,000.00
1945	Portland Open Invitational	2	71	71	67	66	275	1,866.66
1945	Tacoma Open	T9	70	71	71	71	283	325.00
1945	Seattle Open	1	62	68	63	66	259	2,000.00
1945	Glen Garden Invitational	1	68	69	66	70	273	2,000.00

1945 Earnings $62,437.32

1946

Year	Tournament	Place	R1	R2	R3	R4	Total	Earnings
1946	Los Angeles Open	1	71	69	72	72	284	$2,666.67
1946	San Francisco Open	1	73	70	72	68	283	3,000.00
1946	San Antonio Texas Open	3	64	68	72	69	273	750.00
1946	New Orleans Open	1	73	69	69	66	277	1,500.00
1946	Pensacola Open Invitational	T14	75	69	70	72	286	152.50
1946	St. Petersburg Open	5	68	69	69	71	277	650.00
1946	Miami Four-Ball* (Match Play) (with Jug McSpaden)	T3	Lost in semifinals					300.00
1946	Masters	T7	72	73	71	74	290	356.25
1946	Houston Open	1	70	69	68	68	274	2,000.00
1946	Colonial National Invitational	T9	72	72	71	70	285	520.00
1946	Western Open	T6					280	516.67
1946	Goodall Round Robin	3	+2					1,150.00
1946	U.S. Open	T2	71	71	69	73	284	875.00
1946	Inverness Four-Ball (with Jug McSpaden)	2	+14					850.00
1946	Columbus Invitational	1	72	68	69	67	276	2,500.00
1946	Kansas City Invitational	T3	69	67	68	72	276	1,433.34
1946	Chicago Victory Open	1	73	69	69	68	279	2,000.00
1946	All-American Open	T7	74	72	70	71	287	1,233.34
1946	World Championship of Golf*	2					140	0.00
1946	PGA Championship (Match Play)	T5	Lost in quarterfinals					500.00
1946	Fort Worth Invitational	T7					277	550.00

1946 Earnings $23,503.77

1947

Year	Tournament	Place	R1	R2	R3	R4	Total	Earnings
1947	Masters	T2	69	72	72	70	283	$1,500.00

1947 Earnings $1,500.00

1948

Year	Tournament	Place	R1	R2	R3	R4	Total	Earnings
1948	Masters	T8	71	73	72	74	290	$ 350.00
1948	Colonial National Invitational	6	70	69	73	71	283	800.00

1948 Earnings $1,150.00

1 9 4 9

Year	Event	Pos	R1	R2	R3	R4	Total	Earnings
1949	Bing Crosby Pro-Am*	W/D	76	72			148	$ 0.00
1949	Masters	T8	75	70	74	73	292	311.66
1949	Goodall Round Robin*	4						1,250.00
	1949 Earnings							**$1,561.66**

1 9 5 0

Year	Event	Pos	R1	R2	R3	R4	Total	Earnings
1950	Bing Crosby Pro-Am*	T32	75	74	78		227	$ 0.00
1950	Masters	T4	75	70	69	74	288	720.00
1950	Colonial National Invitational	T27	74	72	76	76	298	0.00
	1950 Earnings							**$720.00**

1 9 5 1

Year	Event	Pos	R1	R2	R3	R4	Total	Earnings
1951	Bing Crosby Pro-Am*	1	71	67	71		209	$2,000.00
1951	Masters	T8	71	73	73	74	291	450.00
1951	Colonial National Invitational	T4	71	71	70	73	285	900.00
	1951 Earnings							**$3,350.00**

1 9 5 2

Year	Event	Pos	R1	R2	R3	R4	Total	Earnings
1952	Bing Crosby Pro-Am*	T16	77	76			153	$ 0.00
1952	Masters	T24	72	75	78	77	302	400.00
1952	Colonial National Invitational	7	74	71	72	71	288	850.00
1952	National Celebrities Open	T2	71	72	67	73	283	1,466.66
1952	Palm Beach Round Robin*	10						600.00
1952	Inverness Round Robin*	5						800.00
	1952 Earnings							**$4,116.66**

1 9 5 3

Year	Event	Pos	R1	R2	R3	R4	Total	Earnings
1953	Bing Crosby Pro-Am*	T15	72	67	75		214	$ 7.14
1953	Masters	W/D	73	73	78		224	0.00
1953	Colonial National Invitational	18	74	73	73	74	294	350.00
1953	Mexican Open*	10	66	72	68	71	277	232.56
1953	Palm Beach Round Robin*	16						400.00
	1953 Earnings							**$989.70**

1 9 5 4

Year	Event	Pos	R1	R2	R3	R4	Total	Earnings
1954	Thunderbird Invitational	W/D	69	69			138	$ 200.00
1954	Masters	T12	73	76	74	73	296	631.25
1954	Ardmore Open	T50	78	71	75	74	298	0.00
1954	Colonial National Invitational	T3	67	74	69	73	283	2,000.00
1954	Palm Beach Round Robin*	T10						575.00
	1954 Earnings							**$3,406.25**

1 9 5 5

Year	Event	Pos	R1	R2	R3	R4	Total	Earnings
1955	Bing Crosby Pro-Am*	W/D	70	75				$ 0.00
1955	Thunderbird Invitational	T20	67	68	74	69	278	192.50
1955	Masters	T10	72	75	74	72	293	695.83
1955	Colonial National Invitational	T12	72	71	73	74	290	593.75
1955	Arlington Hotel Open	T26	74	71	70	72	287	135.00
1955	U.S. Open	T28	77	74	80	75	306	180.00
1955	British Open	T32	72	75	78	71	296	0.00
1955	French Open	1	69	65	67	70	271	1,000.00
	1955 Earnings							**$1,797.08**

1 9 5 6

Year	Event	Pos	R1	R2	R3	R4	Total	Earnings
1956	Bing Crosby National Pro-Am	T45	74	71	78		223	$ 50.00
1956	Thunderbird Invitational*	35	68	71	75	76	290	100.00
1956	Masters	39	73	75	78	80	306	300.00
1956	Colonial National Invitational	T41	70	76	74	82	302	0.00
	1956 Earnings							**$450.00**

* Unofficial PGA Tour event
NA Records not available

1 9 5 7

Year	Event	Pos	R1	R2	R3	R4	Total	Earnings
1957	Thunderbird Invitational*	T32	73	69	72	74	288	$112.50
1957	Masters	T16	74	72	73	76	295	778.75
1957	Colonial National Invitational	T27	76	77	73	70	296	0.00
	1957 Earnings							**$891.25**

1 9 5 8

Year	Event	Pos	R1	R2	R3	R4	Total	Earnings
1958	Bing Crosby National Pro-Am	T53	72	74	73	80	299	$100.00
1958	Jackson Open Invitational*	T2	71	71			142	516.67
1958	Masters	T20	71	77	74	71	293	956.25
1958	Colonial National Invitational	T31	69	76	72	79	296	0.00
	1958 Earnings							**$1,572.92**

1 9 5 9

Year	Event	Pos	R1	R2	R3	R4	Total	Earnings
1959	Bing Crosby National Pro-Am	T28	75	74	69	75	293	$164.55
1959	Thunderbird Invitational*	26	74	70	66	69	279	160.00
1959	Masters	W/D	75	73			148	300.00
1959	Colonial National Invitational	25	76	69	76	72	293	150.00
	1959 Earnings							**$774.55**

1 9 6 0

Year	Event	Pos	R1	R2	R3	R4	Total	Earnings
1960	Masters	CUT	76	76			152	$ 350.00
1960	Colonial National Invitational	T37	72	75	74	73	294	100.00
	1960 Earnings							**$450.00**

1 9 6 1

Year	Event	Pos	R1	R2	R3	R4	Total	Earnings
1961	Seminole Pro-Amateur*	T15	71	76			147	$ 50.00
1961	Masters	T32	71	72	78	77	298	500.00
1961	Waco Turner Open Invitational	T48	73	73	75	76	297	0.00
1961	Colonial National Invitational	43	74	78	69	78	299	100.00
	1961 Earnings							**$650.00**

1 9 6 2

Year	Event	Pos	R1	R2	R3	R4	Total	Earnings
1962	Bing Crosby National Pro-Am	T15	71	75	71	76	293	$ 760.00
1962	Masters	T33	72	76	72	76	296	500.00
1962	Colonial National Invitational	T17	73	70	74	73	290	750.00
	1962 Earnings							**$2,010.00**

1 9 6 3

Year	Event	Pos	R1	R2	R3	R4	Total	Earnings
1963	Masters	CUT	79	77			154	$ 600.00
1963	Colonial National Invitational	T48	76	77	73	74	300	150.00
	1963 Earnings							**$750.00**

1 9 6 4

Year	Event	Pos	R1	R2	R3	R4	Total	Earnings
1964	Masters	CUT	75	76			151	700.00
	1964 Earnings							**$700.00**

1 9 6 5

Year	Event	Pos	R1	R2	R3	R4	Total	Earnings
1965	Masters	T15	70	74	72	74	290	$1,300.00
1965	Junior League of Tulsa Pro-Am*	T11						NA
1965	Colonial National Invitational	58	78	72	74	78	302	150.00
	1965 Earnings							**$1,450.00**

1 9 6 6

Year	Event	Pos	R1	R2	R3	R4	Total	Earnings
1966	Masters	CUT	76	78			154	$1,000.00
1966	Colonial National Invitational	W/D	75				75	$0.00
	1966 Earnings							**$1,000.00**

The Nelson Record in Major Tournaments

MASTERS TOURNAMENT

Year	Place	Score	To Par	1st	2nd	3rd	4th	Earnings
1935	T-9	291	+3	71	74	72	74	$ 137.50
1936	T-13	298	+10	76	71	77	74	50.00
1937	1	283	-5	66	72	75	70	1,500.00
1938	5	290	+2	73	74	70	73	400.00
1939	7	287	-1	71	69	72	75	250.00
1940	3	285	-3	69	72	74	70	600.00
1941	2	283	-5	71	69	73	70	800.00
1942	1	280	-8	68	67	72	73	1,500.00
1946	T-7	290	+2	72	73	71	74	356.25
1947	T-2	283	-5	69	72	72	70	1,500.00
1948	T-8	290	+2	71	73	72	74	350.00
1949	T-8	292	+4	75	70	74	73	311.00
1950	T-4	288	+0	75	70	69	74	725.00
1951	T-8	291	+3	71	73	73	74	450.00
1952	T-24	302	+14	72	75	78	77	400.00
1953	T-29	297	+9	73	73	78	73	200.00
1954	T-12	296	+8	73	76	74	73	631.25
1955	T-10	293	+5	72	75	74	72	695.83
1956	39	306	+18	73	75	78	80	300.00
1957	T-16	295	+7	74	72	73	76	778.75
1958	T-20	293	+5	71	77	74	71	956.25
1959	WD	148	+4	75	73			300.00
1960	CUT	152	+8	76	76			350.00
1961	T-32	298	+10	71	72	78	77	500.00
1962	T-33	296	+8	72	76	72	76	500.00
1963	CUT	156	+12	79	77			600.00
1964	CUT	151	+7	75	76			700.00
1965	T-15	290	+2	70	74	72	74	1,300.00
1966	CUT	154	+10	76	78			1,000.00

Masters played in: **29**

Rounds played in: **107**

Times finished 72 holes: **24**

Scoring Average: **73.15**

Relation to Par: **+126**

Top 3 Finishes: **5**

Top 5 Finishes: **7**

Top 10 Finishes: **14**

Top 25 Finishes: **20**

Rounds in 60s: **9**

Rounds under par: **27**

Rounds at par: **17**

Rounds over par: **63**

Lowest Masters Score: **66**

Highest Masters Score: **80**

Earnings: **$18,141.83**

U.S. OPEN

Year	Place	Score	To Par	1st	2nd	3rd	4th	Earnings
1934	CUT	162	+22	79	83			$ 0.00
1935	T-32	315	+27	75	81	82	77	0.00
1936	CUT	153	+9	79	74			0.00
1937	T-20	295	+7	73	78	71	73	50.00
1938	T-5	294	+10	77	71	74	72	412.50
1939	1	284	+8	72	73	71	68	1,000.00
1940	T-5	290	+2	72	74	70	74	325.00
1941	T-17	297	+17	73	73	74	77	50.00
1946	2	284	+-4	71	71	69	73	875.00
1949	CUT	151	+9	74	77			1,500.00
1955	T-28	306	+26	77	74	80	75	180.00

Events played in: **11**

Rounds played in: **42**

Times finished 72 holes: **8**

Scoring Average: **74.14**

Relation to Par: **+133**

Top 3 Finishes: **2**

Top 5 Finishes: **4**

Top 10 Finishes: **4**

Top 25 Finishes: **6**

Rounds in 60s: **2**

Rounds under par: **7**

Rounds at par: **3**

Rounds over par: **32**

Lowest U.S. Open Score: **68**

Highest U.S. Open Score: **83**

Earnings: **$2,892.50**

(Left) Early Masters Champions in 1947: Byron ('37 and '42), Henry Picard ('38), Jimmy Demaret ('40), Craig Wood ('41), Gene Sarazen ('35) and Herman Kaiser ('46). Missing is Ralph Guldahl ('39).

(Above) Byron in action at the Masters.

(Facing page) A stellar foursome at Augusta: Byron, President Eisenhower, Ben Hogan and Cliff Roberts.

BRITISH OPEN

Year	Place	Score	To Par	1st	2nd	3rd	4th	Earnings
1937	T-5	296	+8	75	76	71	74	$125.00
1955	T-32	296	+8	72	75	78	71	$0.00

Events played in: **2**
Rounds played in: **8**
Times finished 72 holes: **2**
Scoring Average: **74.00**
Relation to Par: **+16**
Top 3 Finishes: **0**
Top 5 Finishes: **1**
Top 10 Finishes: **1**
Top 25 Finishes: **1**
Rounds in 60s: **0**
Rounds under par: **2**
Lowest British Open Score: **71**
Highest British Open Score: **78**
Earnings: **$125**

PGA CHAMPIONSHIP

1935 – PGA at Twin Hills Country Club,
Oklahoma City, Oklahoma
Shot 80-76; did not qualify for match play
Earnings: $0

1936 – Pinehurst Country Club,
Pinehurst, North Carolina
Shot 80-78; did not qualify for match play
Earnings: $0

1937 – Pittsburgh Field Club,
Aspinwall, Pennsylvania
In the first round, defeated Leo Diegel 2 and 1
In the second round, defeated Craig Wood 4 and 2
In the third round, defeated Johnny Farrell 5 and 4
In the quarterfinals, was beaten by Ky Laffoon 2 up
Earnings: $200

1938 – Shawnee Country Club,
Shawnee-on-Delaware, Pennsylvania
In the first round, defeated Clarence Yockey 5 and 4
In the second round, defeated Al Krueger 1 up 20 holes
In the third round, defeated Harry Bassler 11 and 10
In the quarterfinals, was beaten by Jimmy Hines
2 and 1
Earnings: $250

1939 – Pomonok Country Club,
Flushing, New York
In the first round, defeated Chuck Garringer 4 and 2
In the second round, defeated William Francis 3 and 1
In the third round, defeated Johnny Revolta 6 and 4
In the quarterfinals, defeated Emerick Kocsis 10 and 9
In the semifinals, defeated Dutch Harrison 9 and 8
In the finals, was beaten by Henry Picard 1 up 37 holes
Earnings: $600

1940 – Hershey Country Club,
Hershey, Pennsylvania
In the first round, defeated Dick Shoemaker 4 and 3
In the second round, defeated Frank Walsh 1 up
20 holes
In the third round, defeated Dick Metz 2 and 1
In the quarterfinals, defeated Eddie Kirk 6 and 5
In the semifinals, defeated Ralph Guldahl 1 up
In the finals, defeated Sam Snead 1 up
Earnings: $1,100

1941 – Cherry Hills Country Club,
Cherry Hills, Colorado
In the first round, defeated Bunny Torpey 1 up
In the second round, defeated William Heinlein 1 up
In the third round, defeated Ralph Guldahl 4 and 3
In the quarterfinals, defeated Ben Hogan 2 and 1
In the semifinals, defeated Gene Sarazen 2 and 1
In the finals, was beaten by Vic Ghezzi 1 up 38 holes
Earnings: $600

1942 – Seaview Country Club,
Atlantic City, New Jersey
In the first round, defeated Harry Nettlebladt 5 and 3
In the second round, defeated Joe Kirkwood 2 and 1
In the quarterfinals, defeated Harry Cooper 1 up
39 holes
In the semifinals, was beaten by Jim Turnesa 1 up
37 holes
Earnings: $700

1943 – Manito Golf and Country Club,
Spokane, Washington
In the first round, defeated Mike DeMassey 5 and 4
In the second round, defeated Mark Fry 7 and 6
In the quarterfinals, defeated Willie Goggin 4 and 3
In the semifinals, defeated Charles Congdon 8 and 7
In the finals, was beaten by Bob Hamilton 1 up
Earnings: $1,500

1945 – Moraine Country Club,
Dayton, Ohio
In the first round, defeated Gene Sarazen 4 and 3
In the second round, defeated Mike Turnesa 1 up
In the quarterfinals, defeated Denny Shute 3 and 2
In the semifinals, defeated Claude Harmon 5 and 4
In the finals, defeated Sam Byrd 4 and 3
Earnings: $5,000

1946 – Portland Golf Club,
Portland, Oregon
In the first round, defeated Frank Rodia 8 and 7
In the second round, defeated Larry Lamberger 3 and 2
In the third round, defeated Herman Barron 3 and 2
In the quarterfinals, was beaten by Ed Oliver 1 up
Earnings: $500

Events played: **11**
Qualified for match play: **9**
Matches played: **44**
Wins: **37**
Losses: **7**
Holes played: **1,272**
Times in Semifinals: **6**
Times in Finals: **5**
Championships won: **2**
Earnings: **$10,450**

RYDER CUP

1937 – Southport and Ainsdale Golf Club,
Southport, England
Day One Foursomes: Byron and Ed Dudley defeated
Alf Padgham and Henry Cotton 4 and 2
Day Two Singles: beaten by Dai Rees 3 and 1

Named to the 1939 and 1941 Ryder Cup Teams; not
played because of World War II

1947 – Portland Golf Club,
Portland, Oregon
Day One Foursomes: Byron and Herman Barron
defeated Dai Rees and Sam King 2 and 1
Day Two Singles: Defeated Arthur Lees 2 and 1

Was the non-playing captain in the 1965 matches at
Royal Birkdale Golf Club in Southport, England
USA Team won 19 1/2 to 12 1/2